WHATEVER HAPPENED TO THRIFT?

WHATEVER HAPPENED TO THRIFT?

Why Americans Don't
Save and What to Do
about It

Ronald T. Wilcox

Yale University Press
New Haven & London

Printed in the United States of America.

Library of Congress Cataloging-in-Publication Data
Wilcox, Ronald T.
Whatever happened to thrift? : why Americans don't save and what to do about it / Ronald T. Wilcox.
    p.   cm.
Includes bibliographical references and index.
ISBN 978-0-300-12451-4 (cloth : alk. paper)
1. Saving and investment—United States.   2. Finance, Personal—United States.   I. Title.
HC110.S3W54   2008
332.60973—dc22   2008002493

A catalogue record for this book is available from the British Library.

The paper in this book meets the guidelines for permanence and durability of the Committee on Production Guidelines for Book Longevity of the Council on Library Resources.

10 9 8 7 6 5 4 3 2 1

FOR SHANNON

CONTENTS

ACKNOWLEDGMENTS

Much primary research has contributed to the ideas presented in this book. Those whose ideas were most influential include Brad Barber, Esther Duflo, Thomas Gilovich, Richard Green, Sheena Iyengar, Daniel Kahneman, Terrance Odean, James Poterba, Emmanuel Saez, Richard Thaler, Amos Tversky, and Robert Wright.

Several people read various versions of the manuscript and offered valuable advice. This book is better off for the contributions of these individuals. They include Richard Green, my former colleague at Carnegie Mellon, who first teased me for "wasting my time" writing a book and then proceeded to carefully read the manuscript and offer thoughtful feedback. Kathie Amato, Robert Harris, Shirley Wilcox, and Beth Woods also read early versions of the book and provided useful comments. Andrew King provided diligent and capable research assistance. Michael O'Malley, my editor at Yale University Press, was intellectually engaged in the writing process and this helped considerably.

A substantial portion of this book was written in the summer of 2006, while my wife and I were the long-term guests of her parents, Bill and Jane Indoe. They gave me the physical and mental space to write, for which I am grateful.

The Darden School of the University of Virginia is a unique and venerable institution. Darden's values and culture allowed this book to take shape. While many elite business schools frown upon their faculty writing for nonacademic audiences, Darden encouraged it.

Finally, anyone who has undertaken a large writing project knows that it is basically a selfish act, putting intense periods of work ahead of family and friends. This book took time that my wife, Shannon, and I could have spent together. Its writing spanned the birth of our first child, Tucker, and took time that rightly belonged to them. Thank you, Shannon, for your love and support during this long process.

WHATEVER HAPPENED TO THRIFT?

1

DO AMERICANS SAVE TOO LITTLE?

There is always an easy solution to every human problem—neat, plausible and wrong.
—H. L. Mencken, "The Divine Afflatus" (1917)

This is the story of the average American who has lived well over the past 40 years but now more than ever before lives on borrowed time and money. Americans are the world's prodigal sons, spending all their riches today and guaranteeing themselves a place in the poorhouse of tomorrow. The decline in household savings in the United States is well chronicled in both government statistics and the popular press. In early 2006, commonly cited measures of savings had sunk to levels not seen since the Great Depression, ranking it right at the bottom of the developed world.[1]

So what? Is this really an important enough national issue to garner the kind of press coverage it receives? War in the Middle East is clearly an issue of broad national concern, but personal financial matters are just that—personal. Whether I or my neighbors save enough money to play golf when we retire does not affect anyone but us. So why all the public angst?

Because the U.S. household savings rate does matter. It matters a lot. And your neighbor's saving habits do indeed have important consequences for you personally. There are very good reasons why, if Americans save too little, we will be worse off in the future, both individually and collectively. For example, our ability to maintain the high standard of living we have historically enjoyed will be diminished. Our ability to create and implement national- and world-improving technologies will fade. The arts, which from time immemorial have relied on private wealth, will struggle. Even our ability to provide for national defense will be affected. Like any vibrant democracy, we argue about how to spend our wealth, what proportion of it should be left in the hands of private citizens, how much should be controlled by the state, what should be spent to support the arts, and how much should be spent to field an effective military. But these are good problems to have. National wealth, at both the public and private levels, implies the ability to make choices. We want to be able to make those choices.

This book is an unapologetic attempt to reinvent thrift in the United States, to find practical ways to help people consume less and save more now so that we can be a richer people in the future. Magazine and newspaper articles do an able job of excoriating wasteful spending, so we need not squander inordinate space discussing the fact that members of our consumer society dedicate much of their time to, well, consuming. You do not need to read this book to realize that some Americans go crazy with their credit cards—purchasing, for example, a watch accurate to the nanosecond that displays the time in eight different time zones—rather than saving that money for retirement. We all know plenty of people who spend like this. Instead, we use our time here to deeply probe the foundations of the American savings problem, asking "why" more often than "what." Once we have a handle on the causes, we look for meaningful solutions rather than glib admonishments to spend less. We use the results of research in economics, finance, marketing, and psychology to find the ideas that may provide the basis for a broad consensus on how to move forward on the problem of household savings.

In order to do that, we occasionally wade into politics, but not often. With a thorough understanding of the problem, there is much that can be done without raising political ire. Many of the practical ideas and steps that are capable of making real inroads do not emerge from congressional offices and chambers but from the meeting rooms of U.S. employers, both large and small. Businesspeople are the sharp edge of the proverbial spear in the battle to make thrift "a permanent and happy habit of the American people."[2]

There is no magic bullet here, no simple, elegant, and all-encompassing solution of the sort that Mencken would deride. Instead we have a patch-work of ideas emerging from many different places and intellectual traditions, located in the often-hidden common ground of economists, sociologists, and psychologists, where hope for real and practical solutions lies. These streams of thought jointly tell a fascinating tale that shows how our difficulty in savings is caused not merely by the commercial environment of the times but also by the history of our nation, its current place in the world economy, and ancient thought patterns that have evolved over hundreds of thousands, if not millions, of years. All these underlying reasons play a role in disrupting savings, and we must be aware of them if we want to find solutions that will really work in the long run.

We begin by clarifying what it means to save "too little." Is this just a matter of the "damned lies" that statistics can tell, or is there really something going fundamentally wrong in the United States with regard to household savings?[3]

The question of whether Americans save too little can be couched in purely economic terms. Private savings not only provide the basis of future consumption for the individual but also are important for growth in the entire economy. Household savings form a pool of money that businesses can borrow from to invest in technologies, from the next great heart medication to a new way of dusting, that improve our standard of living. Lack of savings implies both risks to the individual and potentially higher borrowing costs for businesses that choke off advancements in productivity and social welfare. Although these purely economic arguments comprise the bulk of the academic work in this area, they tell only part of the story. Many Americans who read and hear about historically low savings rates infer a moral tale: a nation spending beyond its means, trapped by the lure of consumerism and behaving like the biblical prodigal son.[4] The message strikes as much at our own mythology and self-perceptions as it does at the optimal level of capital formation. Both public policy and personal values are at play in this issue. Most of this chapter explores the economic arguments for determining whether the rate at which Americans save is indeed too low. If there is a moral tale here, we provide its economic context rather than its narrative.

What Does "Saving Too Little" Really Mean?

At the level of the individual household, saving too little implies insufficient financial resources to cope with unexpected events. In noneconomic speak, it means there is not enough money in the bank to maintain our standard of living should we, for instance, lose our jobs or get sick. We might reasonably call these "expected unexpected" events. Although at any given time we do not expect to lose our jobs, we know that there is a significant chance it will happen over the course of a working lifetime.[5] Similarly, on any given morning we do not expect to get sick, but we realize that it will probably happen at least a few times over the years. Sickness can generate immediate and substantial income losses, particularly for those workers who are not salaried and depend on hourly wages. Savings provide the cushion we need when these kinds of events occur.

Saving too little at the individual level also has consequences for retirement. Government-sponsored pension plans do not provide most people with adequate funding for a comfortable retirement. In today's economy, they do not even come close. Those who rely solely on Social Security for their well-being in retirement draw monthly checks that at best provide a very meager existence. Individuals must look to private sources such as their own savings or assets accumulated in an employer-sponsored pension plan to help fund retirement.

Are we saving enough? The standard economic view is that at any given time a person has well-defined preferences that stipulate whether he or she will choose to save some portion of a monthly paycheck or spend it all. In other words, people know exactly what they want and what they do not want. In that sense, the savings of any given household is a direct outcome of its members' personal preferences. Economists see these preferences as the sacrosanct realm of the individual. If someone is in debt up to the eyeballs, it is because that person prefers to discount future consumption very heavily relative to current consumption. One may believe that, for whatever reason, it is much better to buy the new car and new clothes now than to worry about the future, if it ever shows up. Many economists believe, then, that savings is a matter of individual choice, and questions about "too much" or "too little" have a moral punch that is not relevant to the decision making of rational people. Who are we to question what this or that person wants out of life?

As it turns out, many individuals worry about their lack of savings. A survey conducted in 2002 indicated that 68% of workers thought their savings rate was too low.[6] It is difficult to scan the radio without coming across at least one call-in show geared toward helping people get out of debt and save more money. The decidedly libertarian view of modern economic thought states that people generally know what is best for themselves with respect to consumption and savings decisions. Even if we take this view, the fact that many people report feeling uncomfortable with their level of savings and seek ways to increase it should give us pause. Perhaps it is not so foolish after all to ask the rather paternalistic question: "Is a given household saving too little?"[7]

Those who study savings often ask whether the pool of household savings in the United States is sufficient to fuel economy-wide growth or sustain overall standards of living rather than focusing on analogous individual-level questions. Many popular publications and media outlets have already concluded that the U.S. household savings rate is exceedingly low, but is that really true? Are there reasons why the paucity of household savings may look worse than it actually is? We begin our discussion of savings with a brief examination of this question, as it is fundamental to the rest of this chapter and indeed the rest of the book. If you are not an economist, don't watch C-SPAN for entertainment; if you would rather not talk about realized versus unrealized capital gains at parties, you may want to read the next section at bedtime. It is an essential section, however, since it is the intellectual basis for the question being probed in this book. And, if you are ever a contestant on the game show *Jeopardy!* and see "The measure of U.S. savings that includes the purchase of consumer durables," you can add to your winnings by asking, "What is the U.S. Federal Reserve's Flow of Funds measure?"

Measuring Household Savings

At its most basic level, the savings of an individual household is simply the difference between what a household earns over a given period of time and what it consumes during that time. If the members of that household earn more than they consume, they are net savers, and if the reverse is true, they are net debtors. A household saves so that it may increase consumption in the future, protect against future uncertainties in income, and provide bequests upon the death of its members. The most widely quoted gauge of household savings is the U.S. Department of Commerce's National Income and Product Accounts (NIPA) measurement, which uses accounting rules to determine what counts as savings and what does not. On the surface, this determination might seem easy, but it is not. For example, if a household owns stock, should the dividends from that stock be counted as part of that household's savings? What about capital gains? Should money contributed to Social Security be counted as savings, even though it is unclear how much of it will be returned to the contributor in the future and how much of it will be used to offset national deficits? Are housing costs consumption or investment? Your answer to this question might depend on the trajectory of housing prices. In a period of prolonged upward price movements, many Americans view their homes as investments, but would the same hold true if prices flattened or even declined for a substantial period of time?

NIPA has been widely criticized for the way it measures household savings.[8] Indeed, some of the rules it uses to classify savings seem to omit a great deal of what many of us would include. For example, stock dividends are counted as household income, but both unrealized and realized capital gains are not. Thus the equity boom of the 1990s and the increased household wealth that followed were largely ignored by the NIPA household savings metric. Likewise, the net acquisition of owner-occupied housing is included in savings, but both realized and unrealized capital gains from housing that has appreciated are not. While there are other grounds on which to question the completeness of the picture NIPA provides about household savings, these two—the treatment of capital gains derived from equities and real estate—are most salient. Few would argue that Americans treated the unrealized capital gains from stock holdings as a store of wealth in the 1990s, and in the current market, few would doubt that Americans look to the gains in the value of their homes as an important part of their personal balance sheet. NIPA, it seems, may do a good job gauging the portion of wages that are spent and saved, but it is not good at judging changes in household wealth.

Another measurement of household savings is the Flow of Funds (FOF), put out by the Board of Governors of the Federal Reserve System. An important difference between the NIPA measure and the FOF approach is that the FOF includes the purchase of consumer durables (a new dishwasher, for example) as a form of savings, while NIPA does not. FOF also includes realized capital gains from stocks and other appreciated assets in the household income calculation. Taken in totality, FOF indicates household savings rates that are mostly greater over time than those suggested by NIPA, but recently, the opposite has been true. A recent NIPA measure of household savings, for Quarter 2 of 2006, was −0.7% of disposable income, while the FOF metric stood at 2.3%. The story NIPA tells is that the average household spends more than it earns, while the FOF measurement indicates a very small amount of savings.

Neither of these saving metrics, however, includes unrealized capital gains, which is actually quite a salient factor. Depending on the locality, housing markets in the United States ranged from mild appreciation to an outright boom between 2000 and 2005. This real estate bull market was in no way confined to major cities. Housing prices in Charlottesville, Virginia, for example, rose about 50% between 2002 and 2005. Even in the 2006–2007 downturn in the housing market, many people still held considerable wealth in the value of their homes. If home owners plan to downsize their housing as they age, it would seem entirely reasonable for them to count unrealized real estate–based wealth when determining how much savings they will need for retirement.

These metrics are probably best understood by examining how they vary over time. Figure 1.1 depicts both the NIPA and FOF measures of the household savings rate from 1975 through the first quarter of 2006.

Despite their deficiencies, the trend in NIPA and FOF measurements points to the same basic conclusion. While the precise metrics may be open to criticism, the overall conclusion that U.S. household savings have fallen precipitously over the past two decades is solid.[9] Americans currently appear to be saving far less than they have historically, and the NIPA figures taken at face value indicate that the savings rate has not been this low since the Great Depression.[10]

If we apply these same metrics to the rest of the world, how does the United States measure up? Answer: We save less than anyone in the

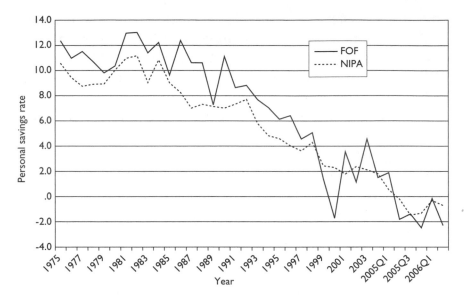

Figure 1.1: Savings as measured by the National Income and Product Accounts (NIPA) and Flow of Funds (FOF)
Source: Author, based on data provided by the Federal Reserve Board and the Bureau of Labor Statistics.

developed world, period. Americans save less from their paychecks than the Japanese, and far less than Europeans, even though government-sponsored pensions are more generous in Europe and Japan.[11] Americans are responsible for more of their economic well-being in old age but are less likely to be prepared for it.

Despite imperfect measures of household savings and international comparisons, we nonetheless can say with confidence that U.S. households are saving far less of their regular take-home pay than they have at any time in recent history. It is much harder to say with equal conviction whether Americans' current wealth accumulations, both realized and unrealized, are sufficient for their long-term financial well-being. No one knows whether the housing market will continue to cool over the next few years or whether it will rebound. No one knows what the level of the stock market will be in, say, 10 years. We may talk about it over the fence with our neighbors or read the premonitions of soothsayers, but in the end there is a great deal of uncertainty in these markets. Even without knowledge of what the future holds, however, there are disturbing trends that foreshadow an insufficiency of savings.

Most of us budget our monthly expenses based on income earned from work, and we tend to consume most of the money we take in. If asset prices suddenly fell or resumed a modest rate of appreciation, people would have to allocate additional wages to their savings to make up for the capital gains they had been experiencing. This would be necessary to maintain the same trajectory of wealth accumulation and their future standard of living. However, cutting back on monthly expenditures in order to save more from wages would be so psychologically painful for many households that we can reasonably doubt it would occur. Once you have digital cable and high-speed Internet service, it is hard to give them up. When you eat out three nights a week, it is difficult to cut down to only once a week. While common economic models of optimal household savings do not differentiate between wealth earned through asset price appreciation and wealth earned through setting aside some income, these two types of savings have very distinct psychological effects. We return to this idea at length in Chapter 3, but suffice it to say that the current state of U.S. household savings is fragile at best. Economists may disagree on whether the current rate of asset accumulation among households is sufficient to maintain standards of living in retirement, but the vulnerability of this current rate seems abundantly clear. U.S. households are at risk for significant financial shortfalls.

The Acute Risk for Poorer Americans

The risk of falling short financially is particularly critical for households of modest means. When we talk about sufficiency of savings, we often couch it in terms of a household's ability to replicate its working income. For example, standard bits of financial advice might be (1) "you should have enough savings to withstand a six-month period of unemployment" or (2) "your retirement savings should be enough to generate income equal to 80% of your preretirement salary." Both of these rules tie one's advised level of savings to one's employment income. They acknowledge that we cannot expect those of more modest means to save as much in absolute terms as wealthier Americans, and they are designed to ensure that households have ample savings to withstand drops in their current levels of income without severely undermining their lifestyles. For example, if you do not drive a Jaguar now, it is probably not terribly important to your personal happiness that you drive one during a period of unemployment or when you retire. But if you are the Jaguar-driving type, you may consider it quite important to keep your Jag rather than trade it in for a used Toyota. It is the nature of the human condition that we tend to enjoy things more if we view them as upgrades instead of downgrades.[12] Giving up goods we have come to enjoy is not greeted with much cheer. It is possible, then, to rephrase our question about the sufficiency of household savings in psychological terms: Are households—and particularly households of more modest means—saving enough for their future happiness? Discouragingly, they are not. Using data that contains much more detail on household finances than the aforementioned NIPA or FOF, Karen Dynan of the Federal Reserve Board and two academic economists, Jonathan Skinner and Stephen Zeldes, in 2004 looked at savings rates across households with different incomes. The disparity in savings was startling (table 1.1).[13]

In table 1.1, "Active Savings" is a measure of how much is saved from current income, netting out items such as house price appreciation and stock price gains. This measure answers the simple question, "How much of your paycheck do you set aside as savings?" These results apply to people aged 40 to 49; researchers found that those who are somewhat younger tend to save a little less and those who are a little older save a bit more, but income is a far better predictor of savings rate than age, so the

Table 1.1: The Relationship between Savings Rates and Income in People Aged 40 to 49

	Active Savings	*Active Savings + Pension*
Income Quintile 1	1%	9%
Income Quintile 2	3%	14%
Income Quintile 3	6%	17%
Income Quintile 4	7%	19%
Income Quintile 5	14%	24%

Note: Income Quintile 1 indicates households in the lowest 20% of U.S. household incomes; Quintile 2 represents households in the 20–40% range, and so forth.
Source: Dynan, Skinner, and Zeldes (2004), table 3, p. 416.

table represents general savings rates. The second column shows the savings rate when you add the active savings rate from the first column to wealth accumulated in private and public pension plans (that is, 401(k)s and Social Security). The rich undoubtedly save a much higher portion of their income than the poor; Dynan, Skinner, and Zeldes found savings rates exceeding 50% among some very wealthy individuals. They checked this qualitative result using a number of different savings measures, and the basic result continued to hold. Since 2004, overall savings rates have continued to fall. We can be confident that there is a wide disparity between how the rich and poor save, and we can also be reasonably sure that the active savings rates among the poorest quintile of American households is now negative. It is pretty clear that negative savings rates are not part of the golden road that leads to any reasonable definition of economic "happiness."

Counterintuitive as it might sound, mainstream economic analyses of household savings and consumption decisions often have assumed that both wealthy and poorer households would end up saving about the same proportion of their lifetime income.[14] It is logical that people who are saving money now to maintain their standard of living in the future would save about the same proportion of their lifetime income regardless of what that income might be. For example, if you need to generate $30,000 per year in investment income to maintain your standard of living, your individual savings would have to be about $600,000.[15] Similarly, if you need $100,000 per year, about $2 million in savings will be necessary. In other words, stable consumption over time requires that a certain proportion of income is saved rather than an absolute dollar amount. As straightforward as this assumption may seem, it is unrealistic in today's world. The behavior we see in our everyday lives stands in stark contrast to the proscriptions of formal economic theory and folk wisdom.

Poorer Americans typically save and accumulate assets in ways that are markedly different from those of their wealthier counterparts. The poor concentrate their asset holdings in items such as checking accounts and automobiles rather than in financial assets such as stocks and bonds.[16] Figure 1.2 shows the level of participation in several classes of assets among households with varying amounts of wealth. One of the more striking results of this analysis—as well as other similar examinations[17]—is that

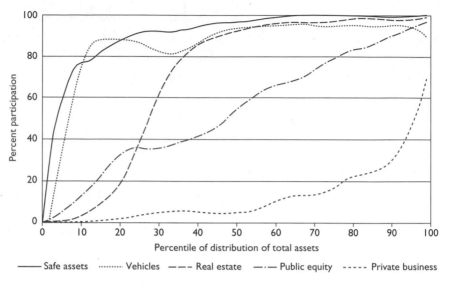

Figure 1.2: Asset holdings among richer and poorer U.S. households
Source: Campbell (2006).

poorer households do not hold the kinds of financial assets with the potential for higher returns. This finding is seen most directly in the scarcity
of publicly traded equity (stocks) in the asset holdings of poorer and even
middle-income households. Poor people simply do not own stocks, or
pooled investment accounts that might invest in stocks (mutual funds),
with any degree of frequency. Whatever money they do have is much
more likely to sit in a checking or low-interest-bearing transaction account. Given that equities provide a much greater potential for long-term
growth in wealth than do checking accounts, it is of great concern not
only that poorer Americans save little but also that their meager savings
are being stored and invested in a way that virtually guarantees they will
remain poor.

Economy-wide Considerations

While there is considerable evidence that a substantial proportion
of individual U.S. households are saving too little to ensure their future
consumption needs, the evidence that domestic economic growth is being

stifled by decreased access to capital is less clear. Savings are important to the economy because companies, both large and small, often need to borrow money to grow. Very few businesses bring in enough money to make payroll, purchase inventory, and pay their other bills immediately—the initial shortfall must be paid by someone. Even mature businesses may issue debt or borrow to fund growth opportunities.

For businesses that start small and plan on staying small (for example, many restaurants) the shortfall may be paid out of the owner or operator's savings. Small businesses may also seek bank financing in which the bank offers a loan in exchange for a payment plan and perhaps some collateral. A particularly promising start-up company may seek funding from a small group of wealthy individuals, or "angels," to finance the early stages of its business, or it may look to investment companies that pool monies of investors and institutions to fund later stages of business growth. U.S. financial markets are nearly legendary for their ability to match dollars with opportunities. Basically, however, all funding is derived from someone's savings. If a new business owner has no savings, he or she cannot individually fund the initial shortfall the business will likely generate. If no one puts money in the bank, the bank cannot loan it out. If there are no wealthy individuals who do not use all of their income for consumption, there can be no angels. Likewise, a large company that issues bonds to pay for a new factory needs people to buy the bonds. Capital, and the growth that flows from the access to capital, requires savings of some kind. That statement is as close as they come to a pure mathematical identity in the world of economics. No savings equals no available capital; no available capital equals lost opportunity for growth.

The good news for American businesses is that there have been and remain plenty of people outside of the United States who are willing to purchase dollar-denominated debt. That is, they are saving money and are willing to let American companies and the U.S. government borrow it. About half of the debt issued by the U.S. government is held by foreign governments and foreign nationals. Japan's holdings of $668 billion are more than double that of the second-place finisher, China, which holds $262 billion.[18] The United States is such an attractive place to invest because it has, among other attributes, a highly developed and transparent legal system and the resultant ability to enforce business contracts,[19] a stable political regime with a low level of endemic corruption, a well-developed transportation and communication infrastructure, a reasonably well-educated workforce, labor laws that are favorable to business compared with those in the rest of the developed world, and highly liquid and easy-to-access markets for the U.S. dollar and dollar-denominated assets. For all our hand-wringing, talk of problems, and grumbling about the United States, we remain the nation of choice for business and investment. The wealth of individuals and governments from around the world still regularly heads westward across the North Atlantic and eastward across the Pacific. It flows into the skyscrapers of Lower Manhattan and the soap manufacturers of Cincinnati.

As a nation, we are a profound anomaly in the apparent lack of any link between domestic savings and availability of investment capital. The general rule is that domestic savings provide the long-term stable funding for domestic enterprises, and even in our world of global capital flows, long-term departures from this model are rare.[20] Americans stand alone in our ability to consistently attract investment capital that far exceeds our domestic savings. That fact alone should give us some pause. If world capital markets suddenly decided that the United States was not the best place to invest and we had to rely on domestic savings alone for funding, there is little question that household savings could not immediately fill the void. Interest rates would rise and domestic growth would slow, perhaps precipitously. While our attractiveness as a haven for investment monies has allowed our economy to grow unencumbered despite capital shortages, it is completely reasonable to ask whether this situation can persist. I think it is irrelevant to ask exactly how long it will persist. The more interesting question is whether there are real risks on the horizon that could cause domestic household savings to be the dominant source of investment capital for the U.S. economy.

Of course, there are risks; some of them are tied to subtle macroeconomic market mechanisms such as the reaction of currency exchange rates to the U.S. Federal Reserve interest rate policy. These kinds of traditional economic effects have been discussed at length elsewhere. However, a thorough knowledge of economic laws or theorems is not required to understand some risks that are very present and very real. What if a terrorist organization successfully executed a large attack within the United States?

In our post–September 11 world, this is a real possibility. Even if the actual damage inflicted by such an attack was not sufficient to cause economic disruption, such an assault could shake international confidence in the United States as a safe haven for investment. So much as a temporary pause in the liquidity of our financial markets, in the ability of foreigners to get their money out of the United States and back into their own bank accounts, could have a devastating effect on the ability of the United States to attract investment capital. If the attack did cause major economic disruption, it would be that much worse. What if the next few hurricane seasons were to result in several landfalls in or near major cities, causing extensive damage?[21] Although hurricane damage to urban areas occurs infrequently, major cities in the U.S. Northeast are susceptible to hurricanes. Overall economic activity could experience a sizable downturn and government deficits could rise further to deal with the recovery—both would be negatives to a foreign investor looking for opportunities. Potential crises such as a broadening of the war in the Middle East, another Enron-type scandal, or a flu pandemic could trigger a repatriation of capital (economic-speak for people taking their money back to their home countries). In such a situation, the U.S. economy would in many respects be the most dramatically affected in the world.

The strongest counterargument for this troubling macroeconomic scenario was posed to me by George David, CEO of United Technologies.[22] I had occasion to speak with him one afternoon about the U.S. savings rate and its implications for domestic businesses. He was skeptical that the low savings rate would choke off growth because in his own businesses, largely manufacturing-based concerns, the need for capital was shrinking rapidly owing to productivity advances. Citing the performance of Otis Elevator, a United Technologies company, he noted, "We now make three times as many elevators with less capital and 9% less labor than we used to. Increased productivity solves the savings problem." This argument is a powerful one for manufacturing companies. Their need for capital can indeed be dramatically reduced with gains in production efficiency. It is less applicable for service-based companies, an increasing part of the U.S. economy, where the current capital requirements are low and room for capital efficiency improvements are scant. Perhaps the shift from a production-oriented economy to a service-oriented economy will cushion the impact that the lack of domestic savings has on the ability of businesses to raise capital as less-capital-intensive businesses replace their more-capital-intensive counterparts. That shift may allow us some time for the savings rate to recover before it has the potential to make a substantial impact on the economy.

Is There a Problem?

I think there is a big problem. While those who predict a near-term crisis are probably overstating the case, the horizon holds both risks of large, economy-wide problems and near certainties of hardship for many U.S. households. Unless many Americans make substantial changes in their savings and consumption behaviors, they are in for a rude awakening later in life. Macroeconomic events could arouse us sooner rather than later, but we can be reasonably sure that a day of reckoning will come. In addition to the continual and often poorly reasoned reminders that we read in the popular press, we need some practical steps to take to ameliorate this crisis. Some of these steps will necessarily be based on public policy, but there are powerful ways that the private sector can step up as well. Before I dispense advice, however, it is important that we understand why this problem has arisen. We also need to have a firm grasp on how people handle their money, the psychological mistakes they often make, and what they are doing with their savings. The whys and hows of household finance are paramount; from them we can derive a practical set of ideas that are less about political rhetoric and more about real solutions.

2

WHY AMERICANS DON'T SAVE ENOUGH

We are now reasonably sure that, on average, Americans save too little, and this is particularly the case among the less prosperous. And we know that Americans themselves are worried about it. These facts together offer a riddle of sorts: If we know there is a problem, why do we still save too little money to provide for our future needs? Describing behavior is easier than probing its causes. But probing is exactly what we do here, not only because it is useful for an in-depth understanding of the issue itself but because it will help us when we begin to explore some practical solutions.

There are many "cocktail theories" that attempt to explain why Americans save too little: Americans like their big cars and houses too much. Americans cannot stay away from credit cards. Americans work too much and substitute consumption for the absence of leisure time. We all have probably heard some of these theories and perhaps have come up with a few of our own. This chapter discusses the set of reasons that have the most and least merit regarding our poor record of saving. I have conducted basic research in this area and am familiar with the research of others whose results speak directly or indirectly to this complex issue. Some of the research is older, classic material while other ideas are right at the leading edge of their respective disciplines.

In the next two chapters, we draw together research from economists, psychologists, and even the occasional biologist and astronomer in an attempt to understand why Americans save so little and why so many of us make bad decisions with our money. And we tell lots of stories—about shopping and buying and the many little thoughts and consumer activities that fill our daily lives.

We begin, however, by discussing two very common cocktail theories of overconsumption.

Easy Access to Consumer Credit

Credit cards. If ever there was a genuine cocktail theory of why Americans don't save, this is it! The credit card offers that flood our mailboxes, both physical and electronic, will be mentioned within the first 60 seconds of any conversation about why Americans save so little. I have been the recipient of many invited and uninvited theories on the causes of low U.S. household savings. Based on my unscientific sampling, credit card companies are widely viewed as the villains: they tempt us with their offers and we are helpless before their siren song.

We tend to think of credit as a modern-day phenomenon, but it is decidedly not. Taking on debt to finance future financial gain and even current consumption is an ancient idea. The Babylonians had detailed laws for dealing with debt contracts. The Greeks and Romans both used credit extensively to finance far-flung commercial ventures. Trade ships needed credit to purchase their cargoes and made contracts to repay loans once the cargo was transported and sold.[1] They also extended loans for personal consumption, but with rather harsh terms. Instead of the cushion of modern bankruptcy laws, more ancient forms of delinquent debt collection involved selling the debtor into slavery.

Credit cards are simply the latest incarnation of a consumer debt contract—also called an installment loan, which is a financial instrument that has been an integral part of the U.S. economy since the early twentieth century. After World War I, the proliferation of consumer products and a liberal regulatory environment combined to make buying on "payments" an accepted part of American family finances.[2] Refrigerators, washing machines, sewing machines, and many other new technologies that graced the homes of middle-class households were acquired with credit. Americans, it appears, have had little moral angst about buying now and paying later for quite some time.

The regulatory environment of the United States allows for the easy construction of consumer debt contracts. In most countries, however, individuals are not as free to enter into debt contracts. There is little evidence, for example, that Japanese consumers do not want access to consumer debt instruments such as credit cards, but Japanese banks were not allowed to offer revolving credit until the 1990s; even then, the types of offers available were generally both unattractive and difficult to use.[3] Similar historic restrictions can be found in other developed nations as well. The upshot is that credit card usage varies considerably, even across highly developed economies, with the United States and Canada leading the way, for reasons more historical than cultural.[4]

Credit cards are more an effect than a cause. Our mailboxes are full of credit card offers because we want them. Companies that market credit cards must think very carefully before they put a glossy, well-designed credit card offer in the mail. Those gold-embossed offers cost them a lot of money and they will not produce and mail them unless they know they can acquire a certain number of new customers. Much like the "tin men" of the 1950s, they will not show up unless they think they can make a buck. Our ability to figure out who will actually accept a credit card offer has evolved since then. Academics and businesses now use very sophisticated models to determine what probability the American Express offer that shows up in your mailbox has of finding a willing customer.[5] There are now well-respected academic journals in marketing whose purpose is to "answer important research questions in marketing using mathematical modeling," and much of whose intellectual energy and contribution revolves around the mathematical modeling of people's choice processes for goods and services.[6] While it is tempting to believe that the mound of junk mail you receive is the outcome of some thoughtlessly random business process, it is generally far from the case.[7] You are receiving the offer because the vendor expects that you will be more profitable than the average Joe, either because you have demonstrated your willingness to purchase items based on direct-mail marketing in the past or because the vendor believes you have the financial means to make a very large purchase. That is the way this business works.

Even to the extent that credit cards do "cause" some people to get into financial difficulty because of the ease with which credit may be acquired, this is not plausible as a root cause of the U.S. savings problem. Most people are not in trouble with credit card debt. In fact, most Americans handle their credit cards reasonably well, pay their balances on time, and do not get into revolving debt problems.[8] Yet, many of these same people save insufficiently. Blaming the American savings problem on credit cards is like blaming America's obesity problem on McDonald's. It is overly simplistic and does not begin to address the root causes.

To discover what is behind America's abandonment of thrift, we must lift our eyes up from our pile of junk mail and explore what is happening in the U.S. economy, the psychology of the American household, and how the two interact with each other. But first let's examine one more shallow cocktail theory.

Americans Are Overworked by Greedy Corporations

Despite the widespread belief that Americans work more than people in any other nation, it is simply not true. The top prize among Western countries for the highest average number of hours worked in a year goes to Australia. Defying their stereotype as a laid-back, fun-loving nation, Australians work an average of 1,855 hours per year, tops among any Western country that keeps data on labor intensity. Americans and Canadians are not far behind Australians. But, by far, Asians are working the most hours; the top six economies in terms of annual hours worked are all Asian: Thailand (2,228 annual hours per worker), Malaysia (2,244), Hong Kong (2,287), Sri Lanka (2,288), Bangladesh (2,301), and the Republic of Korea (2,447).[9] Data on working hours in mainland China and India are inherently unreliable, but my travels and work in China strongly suggest that working hours there, if properly measured, would also probably trump those in Australia. At least in the cities, the pace of life and work in China is more intense than anything commonly experienced in the United States. Lagging in the field are countries like France and Germany, with noticeably shorter working hours. Americans do work hard, but the idea that we are an anomaly in our work ethic does not square with the data.

Traditionally, economists have viewed labor and leisure as substitutes when an individual makes life activity choices. Rational individuals, rather than nations, make trade-offs between the market wages they can earn through work and how much they enjoy free time. Their taste for leisure time and their preferences for money determine how many hours of labor they supply to the market.

This theory has powerful ability to predict the aggregate amount of labor that will be supplied to the market and how wages will evolve in different economic situations. However, it does a relatively poor job of describing the way most individuals decide how much labor to supply.

Where I teach, my workload is set by the dean of the Darden Graduate School of Business Administration. I cannot go into the dean's office and say, "Bob, I've been thinking that this year I'd like to teach a bit less because I want to take up sailing and spend some time fixing up a boat so that next year my wife and I can sail around the world. Please just pay me a little less this year because I won't be working as hard." It simply does not work that way. I can either choose to teach the load that is set by the dean or I can find a job elsewhere.

That is a pretty typical work situation for most people. You can either work the prescribed amount or quit to find more suitable arrangements such as part-time work. There is no ability to make wage and leisure trade-offs within the context of a given job. Of course, you can try to find another job, but if the basic work situation offered by most employers in terms of work hours and vacation time is about the same, there is little to be gained by searching for a new employer. Therefore, Americans work as much as their bosses tell them to and then spend their earnings freely in the leisure time that remains. Juliet Schor notes this phenomenon in her book, *The Overworked American*, and calls on the federal government to pass laws mandating that employers give their employees more "free time."[10] According to some, greedy U.S. employers are consequently to blame for Americans' hard work and subsequent financial recklessness in their free time. If employers just asked people to work less, so the theory goes, they would not feel compelled to substitute extravagant spending for lack of leisure.

While Schor accurately describes the working situation faced by individual Americans, her arguments fall short in explaining why America's hardworking culture evolved the way it has. In an attempt to explain why Americans work long hours, she critiques modern economic analysis by stating that "firms set the hours they require of their employees," and ridicules the classical economic models in which workers choose their amount of labor and leisure time. In her explanation, she accurately describes the individual decision, but entirely misses the broader social context.[11] Economies of different nations, and even localities within nations, evolve different work intensities based on the willingness of employees to supply or withhold labor. In short, if an employer can find someone who will work longer hours or more productively than someone else for the same amount of money, you can bet that person will get the job. Both the availability of people who can do the job and the basic values of the workers are at play in this labor-supply decision—and those unquestionably vary across countries.

The U.S. economy looks different than that of France because the French consider the value of equality, or egalitarianism, to be very important. French society has therefore constructed laws and societal norms that limit social mobility. In such a system, French workers unsurprisingly see less benefit in working longer hours and consequently are more eager to trade work hours for leisure hours. For Americans, the value of "opportunity" has historically held more sway.[12] Based on this value, laws and social norms allow a high degree of social mobility. Hard work is more likely to generate concrete social and financial benefits, so the marginal worker is more willing to put in a longer work week. Optimism about one's economic opportunities is a fundamental determinant of willingness to work longer hours.[13]

This summer, my wife and I undertook a reasonably large home renovation project. More accurately, we paid a contractor to do it. This is the second major home renovation I have undertaken since first buying a home. My in-laws also hired a contractor recently to do some extensive home maintenance and remodeling work. In each case, I directly observed the work being performed on a day-to-day basis and each time the business model for the contractor was similar in the following way: the owner and the supervisors were white Americans and the labor force was predominantly Latino. Sometimes the Latino workers stayed late in the evening. Sometimes they did not show up until the middle of the afternoon, after they had completed work on another job, and then stayed until about 8:00 p.m. Put succinctly, casual observation suggests that they work extremely long hours, longer than the Americans employed by the same construction companies.[14] Are the contractors forcing their Mexican laborers to work 12- to 14-hour days? Are Mexicans just genetically more hardworking than Americans? The answer, of course, has nothing to do with that. These are immigrants who in many instances are sending money back to relatives in their home countries, money that can make a huge difference in the economic conditions of their families there. They work hard because they see its economic benefit. Many of them would be unhappy if they were forced to work a maximum of 35 hours a week and have six weeks of "free time." The prescription for increased societal happiness advanced by Schor and some other social critics does not hold across cultures and value systems. The value systems of Americans, the French, and Mexican immigrants working in the United States are fundamentally different with respect to the benefits of work.

The reasons for these value differences are as complicated as the histories and economic conditions of the cultures themselves, but we can be sure that some identifiable groups of people work harder than others because of their underlying social preferences, not based on the arbitrary whims of employers. The working conditions offered by employers will—through laws, social norms, and competition for scarce labor—evolve toward the underlying preferences of their potential labor pool. Americans want to work hard, and they want to spend their money, so the labor market obliges. At an individual level, some may not agree with these values, but in many respects, that is quite irrelevant. We are not going to change the American social value of "opportunity" by arguing about it. And it is certainly both difficult and unwise to attempt to outlaw such a basic social construct.

Credit cards and long working hours are two cocktail theories that have one striking similarity: they lay the blame for the paucity of U.S. household savings at the feet of lecherous corporations. This is a convenient lie. Each of us knows how hard it is to psychologically own a problem. It is so much easier to blame someone else. When our problems are someone else's fault, we can continue to feel virtuous and good about ourselves.

But truthfully, we are at the root of the problem; for the most part, it is not the companies, the government, or some evil spirit that possesses us and causes us to spend too much. We are just fallible human beings operating in the world we live in as Americans.

Let's look at the problem with our eyes wide open. Beyond our basic social value of opportunity, what are we thinking and doing that is leading to the savings mess?

Consumption Superdisparity and Surpassing the Joneses

As a professor at a top business school, I belong to what consumer psychology researchers call a particular consumption "reference group."[15] My colleagues, perhaps even more than those who live in my neighborhood, give me cues about what constitutes an appropriate level of consumption for a Darden professor, which is not to say that we all consume the same things. Some of my colleagues drive Porsches and BMWs while others drive Hondas. Some have expansive homes on golf courses while others have smaller homes near the center of Charlottesville. But there are cues nevertheless.

One July morning, very soon after I had joined the Darden faculty, I wandered down the hall in my shorts and sandals. It was summer, after all, and at Carnegie Mellon, my previous employer, a person wearing a clean T-shirt was considered well dressed. One of my colleagues, dressed in Brooks Brothers, stopped to introduce himself. After initial pleasantries, he slowly eyed me from head to foot and quipped, "half pants, half pay." I quickly learned that shorts and sandals were not appropriate dress for the halls of Darden, even in summertime.

I have also picked up many more subtle consumption cues, a few of which follow. For instance, it seems that most of my more senior colleagues have an additional home or homes somewhere outside of Charlottesville. It may be an apartment in Manhattan or a house on the Outer Banks of North Carolina, but they have a place to which they can retreat, particularly in the summer, when energies are less focused on teaching and more focused on research and writing.

It is clearly appropriate for me to purchase a vacation home.

Many of my male colleagues wear coats and ties to school, although the styles are much more likely to be Brooks Brothers or Hickey Freeman than Armani or Versace. There are a few individuals on the faculty who generally dress quite stylishly, but they are in the minority.

I should purchase clothes that are of high quality, but not overly stylish.

The Darden faculty and staff parking lot has clues for what my next car purchase should be. Generally, Darden faculty members drive cars that are nicer than average. Appropriate cars for my next purchase include Toyotas, BMWs, Audis, and especially Volvos. Volvos are part of a universal consumption language among academics; English professors drive old ones, business professors drive new ones. Purchasing a Volvo means that you are smart because Volvo has a reputation of safety, and this makes a nice excuse to own a more expensive car. A Toyota means that you are smart, too, because you have purchased a car known for its reliability and longevity. It also means that you are boring. If you are an assistant professor, you should not buy a Mercedes. People will talk; they will think that you are too enamored with money and you should be spending your time on research rather than zooming around in your expensive car. If you are a more senior professor, a Mercedes is perfectly fine.

I like old Toyota Land Cruisers—the removable hardtop versions that never die—but this is not an appropriate car.

My next car should be a European model or a Toyota. If I would like to be viewed more as a serious intellectual, I should buy a Volvo or a Toyota. If I want to be seen as a financially successful professor, I should purchase a more expensive European make. Forget about American cars. Forget about old Toyota Land Cruisers.

Like most of us, however, my work is only one of the places where I find people who make up my reference group. I live in Charlottesville, Virginia, a city that has many of the same sensibilities as places such as Madison, Wisconsin, or Ithaca, New York. The weather is a little warmer. There are a few more equestrians and a few less not-quite-ex-hippies than in the aforementioned places, but small cities dominated by good universities have a certain uniformity of culture that is evident. From Charlottesville I get clues about what is appropriate. When I do buy my Volvo, I had better not stick my Smith & Wesson bumper sticker on it. Nothing would stand out more in Charlottesville than a gun-oriented bumper sticker that might hint at Republican leanings. A very tasteful, understated "W" with a slash through it would be reference-group appropriate for my Volvo. Also, I should shop at one of the several high-end grocery stores that dot the city. The wholesale warehouse on the outskirts of town is for people of questionable taste. Of course, no one actually tells you these things; you just know them.

We also get consumption information from our friends and family. We choose friends at least in part because they share our basic value systems and they like to do many of the same things that we do in their leisure time. Therefore, our preferences for desired consumption may look quite similar to that of our friends. If we like to go hiking and attend college basketball games, we tend to have friends who do the same. Families, too, are powerful forces. Because siblings often start life in roughly the same socioeconomic circumstances, it is easier for them to compare themselves to each other. They know what possessions their brothers and sisters have and they may want the same for themselves. Colleagues, friends, family, and the town or neighborhood in which we live all form reference points for our consumption decisions.

But something happens with this kind of casual empiricism, when we gather information about what we think is appropriate for us based on conversations with others and our observations of their consumption. We do not remember perfectly. We tend to recall the consumption choices that we like and forget the others more readily. When we see something that pleases us, we take notice and this translates into stronger memories. Over time, our view of what is normal among our reference group shifts to something that is not entirely representative of actual consumption; our memory is biased and constructs a sort of idealized typical. Why does this occur?

Thomas Gilovich, a social psychologist and author, researched the cognitive foundations of this type of selective memory.[16] He argues that the difference between remembering and forgetting information that contradicts your currently held view comes down to whether the data presents itself as the outcome of a "one-sided event" or "two-sided event." A two-sided event is like going fishing and using your favorite lure. Either you catch a fish with it or you do not. This is pretty unambiguous; it is easy to remember whether or not the lure "worked." This is a pure two-sided event, and in situations like this it is not hard to remember outcomes that contradict your initial beliefs. It is not too psychologically onerous to come to reasonably accurate beliefs about the long-run efficacy of different fishing lures.

A one-sided event is quite different in the sense that you only notice the outcome when it turns out a certain way. For example, consider the thought, "I always get a static shock when I touch that sweater." Maybe, but when you touch the sweater and get a shock, you tend to remember that more than when you touch the sweater and nothing happens. When nothing happens, your view of the world does not benefit from accumulating additional information about the nonevent. Over time, your beliefs about the probability that you will get shocked become biased by this asymmetry in memory.

I think most of us experience the consumption behavior of our reference group like Gilovich's one-sided phenomenon. When I walk through the faculty and staff parking lot, I tend to notice the Porsche Boxster more than the Toyota Camry. I pick up on the Audi TT a bit more than the Subaru Outback. When I am invited to one of my colleagues' homes, I notice the mortared bluestone terrace, the English boxwood hedges, and the old heart-of-pine floors. I remember the things I covet more than those I do not. And, over time, my beliefs about what constitutes an appropriate level of consumption for my reference group shift toward extraordinary items that generally are more extravagant and costly than what I currently own.

This shift is helped along by the fact that others often exaggerate a bit when they enthusiastically tell us of their consumption experiences. Have they really eaten at that nice French restaurant as many times as they suggest? Were their seats at the play or the basketball game as good as they claim? Unfortunately, even among friends and family, consumption is exaggerated more often than one would imagine.[17]

This persistent drift in the perception of consumption is the progenitor of financially reckless behavior. Some people are able to tame their wants. Some are able to tolerate an exceptionally material lifestyle because they have the cash flow or wealth to afford it. Many people, however, have desires they want to satisfy but do not have the means. They borrow against the future to have something today, spending every available cent and then some. For example, being highly educated with a low to modest income (that is, overeducated and underpaid) is most likely to cause staggering household debt. Trying to be an active member of the cognoscenti costs money. Your friends attend the openings of art galleries and send their kids to private schools. They eat at posh restaurants and know the difference between good wine and cheap wine. You are asked to attend charitable functions where donations will be expected. This is a socially miserable situation. The world's finer things are all around you, but you have to struggle financially to socialize with your peers, whose well-educated tastes and preferences are probably quite similar to your own. You find yourself wondering which credit card to use or whether you should take out another home equity loan (figure 2.1).

This provides a nice, if not complete, explanation of why it is difficult for some groups to save. But it does not directly address the more pressing question: Is this phenomenon of reference-group distortion and the consequent additional consumption pressure getting worse? Many researchers and authors have concluded that it is worsening, and they have laid the blame at the feet of marketers and advertisers.[18] After all, it is their job to urge us on. Advertising, it is argued, provides constant idealized images of what our reference group is consuming and therefore helps

Income

	Low	High
High Education	Lots of Debt	Moderate Savings
Low	Moderate Savings	High Savings

Figure 2.1: The relationship between income, education, and debt
Source: This matrix was constructed from the results of an argument presented in Schor (1998).

distort our understanding of what constitutes appropriate consumption. I certainly do not dismiss the idea that advertising affects consumption. The advertising industry is a $255 billion industry in the United States for a reason—it works.[19] It is then somewhat of a logical leap to conclude, as this literature does, that advertising affects aggregate consumption in the economy. What advertising does for the sales of one company may be at the expense of another. But I speculate that it does have an aggregate impact and that consumption, particularly luxury consumption, has increased because of advertising.

However, to say that it has an impact does not mean that it is the primary impact. Social critics have been complaining about the effect of advertising on conspicuous consumption at least since the time of Veblen's turn-of-the-nineteenth-century attack on the leisure class.[20] Victorians understood glamour, luxury, and social signaling via consumption perfectly well. We may be a little better now at exploiting these human tendencies and desires for commercial gain, but I do not think we have reached a new world order in which advertising defines our reference groups. For that, we still look to family, friends, and coworkers.[21]

Something has changed in the United States, however, that does have a direct impact on the disparity between what we consume and what we can afford to consume. The distribution of income has shifted and continues to do so. While cries of "the rich are getting richer and the poor are getting poorer" have been part of the U.S. political and economic debate for many years, it is now beyond doubt that changes in the economy over at least the last decade have led to a widening income gap between the nation's richest and poorest, and perhaps even more important for the current issue at hand, between the wealthy and middle class.[22] In 2004, the richest 1% of Americans enjoyed a real income growth of 12.5% while the bottom 99% gained only 1.5%. These figures exclude capital gains from the stock market, so we can assume the disparity in income changes was almost certainly higher than even these numbers suggest.[23] Concentration of income among the wealthiest Americans is approaching levels not seen since the Great Depression. National income has also become more concentrated in the top 5% of income earners, but this change has played out over decades relative to the more recent and rapid concentration among the top 1% of earners. It is an economic phenomenon that is more pronounced in the United States relative to other developed economies. Concerns about the implications of the recent capital concentration are not strictly the bastion of the political Left, but have been voiced by what we might reasonably call mainstream and conservative voices, such as Alan Greenspan:

> [We have a] really serious problem here, as I've mentioned many times before this [U.S. House of Representatives] Committee, in the consequent concentration of income that is rising.[24]

Figures 2.2 and 2.3 were generated from Thomas Piketty and Emmanuel Saez's work on U.S. income distribution. Figure 2.2 depicts the concentration of income for three groups of high-income Americans over the last 90 years. Figure 2.3 compares the historical concentrations of income among the top 0.1% of earners in the United States, France, and the United Kingdom. It is important to remember when you read these graphs that you are looking at income concentration figures, not income levels. For example, in figure 2.2, the solid line indicates the proportion of the entire national income earned by the top 1% of wage earners.

The overall concentration of income among the top 1% has about doubled in the past 30 years, with the last decade seeing sharp increases. Over the past 60 years, there has been a steady increase in income concentration among what we might call the upper middle class or "almost rich" (90–99 fractile). France and the United Kingdom have also seen some increases in concentration over the last 20 years among the top 1%, but these increases are not nearly as dramatic as those in the United States. Particularly among the "super rich," the top tenth of the richest 1%, income concentrations in the United States dwarf those of Western Europe. As the share of national income among higher-income Americans rises, the disparity in the ability to consume among Americans of differing relative economic means also rises.

Herein lies the crux of what I believe is a very important set of circumstances that have led to plummeting savings rates. If you combine the empirical realities that (1) the spread in the income distribution among Americans is becoming larger, (2) an individual's consumption reference group comprises people with varying amounts of income, and (3) memories are asymmetric with respect to consumption observations, what you

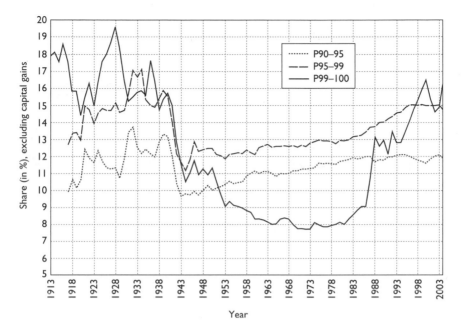

Figure 2.2: Average share of income for households in the 90–95 fractile of income (P90–95), the 95–99 fractile of income (P95–99), and the top 1% of income (P99–100)

Source: Generated from a publicly available data set provided by Piketty and Saez. The data set is available at http://elsa.berkeley.edu/~saez/TabFig2004prcl.xls.

have is a large number of Americans who believe they are not keeping up with their peers. The actual consumption disparity becomes a perceived consumption superdisparity. How this happens is described below.

As income disparities accelerate, I observe some people in my reference group who seem to be able to afford nice things that I do not currently have. Because this observation is a one-sided event, and individuals may exaggerate their own consumption when speaking with others, disparities in remembered consumption accelerate even more quickly than actual disparities. The psychology of memory, the sociology of reference-group communication, and the economics of a widening income distribution combine to form a powerful witches' brew of self-defeating consumption behavior. Actual income disparities, greased by the pervasiveness of marketing communication, are transformed into perceived consumption superdisparities. With such perceived superdisparities, the psychological gap

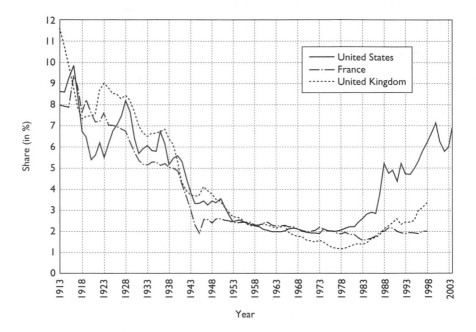

Figure 2.3: The share of national income earned by the top 0.1% of wage earners in the United States, France, and the United Kingdom
Source: Generated from a publicly available data set provided by Piketty and Saez. The data set is available at http://elsa.berkeley.edu/~saez/TabFig2004prel.xls.

in consumption between those with modest incomes and richer Americans exceeds the strict economic differences in their purchasing power. Now I am sure that everyone around me is able to afford the finer things that I cannot. Which credit card should I use?

I believe this is one of the most important reasons for the current downturn in the U.S. savings rate. The reason is not purely economic, sociological, or psychological; it is all of the above. There are, however, other important reasons why saving is uniquely problematic for Americans.

American Optimism

Most mentally healthy people are optimistic about their futures and believe they have more control over events in their lives than they actually have. Ask yourself the simple question, "Do I believe that I can influence the outcome of tossing a pair of dice?" In other words, do you believe that if you *want* to roll snake eyes (a pair of ones) it is more likely that you will? Many people do believe that they have at least some control over the outcome of a roll of the dice or a flip of a coin.[25] In one celebrated example, researchers found that individuals who were able to correctly guess the outcome of a few coin tosses started believing they were better guessers than the average person. These same individuals then became annoyed when they were distracted because distractions might interfere with their concentration and ability to guess correctly.[26] This illusion of control—the belief that one can affect the outcome of demonstrably random events—is widespread in the population but significantly more prevalent among those who have optimistic outlooks on life than those who are pessimistic or in a depressed state. Nature, it seems, endows those who are confident in better tomorrows with the ability to fool themselves into believing that they have more control over many situations than they actually do.[27] Ongoing research in this area of psychology has never conclusively shown which came first—mood or perceived control. Does being depressed make you think that you really cannot control things and that many events in life are random? Or is it the belief that many of life's events are random that makes you depressed? The evidence certainly suggests that these two psychological phenomena are related. If you really are convinced that you have some influence over that slot machine, you are happily incorrect; if you believe it is absolutely random, you are sadly correct.

Optimism is a ubiquitous American trait, the stuff of our mythology and political language. It rode in on the saddles of horses on the Oregon Trail and to California's gold rush. It was Ronald Reagan's "shining city on a hill." It built Manhattan. American optimism is not based on the power and hubris of kings and armies, but on the rising hopefulness of paupers. It is the idea that if I work hard enough, I can trade my rags for riches, or perhaps my children can. No one can tell me otherwise. My forefathers built this country up from the dirt by the sweat of their brow. I can make it.[28] Mark Helprin, a noted columnist and writer, captured the spirit of America's unexpected rise and the basis for American optimism this way:

> This country was not expected to be what it became. It was expected to be infinite seeming in its rivers, prairies, and stars, not in

cities with hundreds of millions of rooms, passages, and halls, and buildings a quarter-mile high. It was expected to be rich in natural silence and the quality of light rather than in uncountable dollars. It was expected to be a place of unfathomable numbers, but of blades of grass and grains of wheat and the crags of mountains rather than millions upon millions of motors spinning and humming at any one time, and wheels turning, fires burning, voices talking, and lights shining. But this great inventory of machines, buildings, bridges, vehicles, and an incomprehensible number of smaller things, is what we have. A nation founded according to a vision of simplicity has become complex. A nation founded with disdain for power has become the most powerful nation.[29]

In Helprin's language, many Americans will find important truths about our country, and those truths give us hope and confidence about who we are as a people.

There is little doubt that this cultural trait, whether innate or learned, has paid dividends for our country. Optimism implies the willingness to take risks, and that willingness not only led to the founding of the nation itself, but is also an important part of the startling success it has enjoyed. Starting a business or investing in one is a risky proposition, but we are all better off because some people take risks; it is vital for economic growth.

Optimism also expresses itself in many different ways at the individual level, from the pervasive belief among younger Americans that the world will generally get better over time to the expectation of good health leading to a longer working career.[30] Relative to the rest of the world, Americans believe that fewer bad things will happen to them. And if we accept the results of psychological research about the illusion of control, Americans not only believe that the world will be good to them, but also that they can change it. A stock will do better because they have invested in it. The company will do better because they are employed there. No need to save money today, because tomorrow they will enjoy a great deal of success! Of course, some of these individuals will turn out to be correct and they will indeed become very successful. We will look at them and tell ourselves that we can be like them if only we work hard enough. And our imperfect memories—made more imperfect still by the media attention garnered by success stories—will retain these images of success, these demigods to which we should aspire. Our spending coincides with our outlook on the future, which trends toward the happy prospect of financial success. If many people feel this way, the government will be obliged to deal with the financially destructive consequences of those who consume like they will become successful, but never do. And what makes matters worse is that some people know it.

The Boomer Vote

Capitalism without failure is like religion without sin.
—Allan Meltzer[31]

We can influence people to make good but difficult choices only if we can credibly precommit to leaving them with the consequences of bad choices.[32] For example, restaurant servers will try to offer their customers good service because they know that at least a portion of their tip depends on it. People pay their taxes because the Internal Revenue Service (IRS) has broad authority to make their life difficult if they do not. Many young adults work hard in school because they believe their employment prospects will be better than if they do not, and they are usually correct in that belief.

But what happens when we take public policy actions that decouple choices and consequences? People continue to build homes and businesses in known floodplains because the federal government offers cheap flood insurance and, moreover, if a disaster strikes, they know that the government will pour money into the area. The leaders of some nations allow rampant political corruption to continue because they know that if their financial situation worsens, the World Bank will ride in on a white horse to help bail them out. And some people do not save enough for their retirement years because they expect the government to help them if things get too difficult.

Baby boomers, born between 1940 and 1964, will be a huge elderly voting bloc, and if historic voting patterns persist, they will vote in large numbers. If many of them are short of money upon retirement, they will pressure their legislators, through organizations such as the American Association of Retired Persons (AARP), to vote for measures that transfer wealth from the people who have saved responsibly to those who have not. Many people who are inclined to save responsibly know this is the case, which begs the question: If I regularly contribute to my employer's 401(k) plan and otherwise take steps to secure my financial future, and if I can expect in return that those who have not saved will get legislation passed so that my Social Security benefits are taxed and theirs are not, then why should I save?

American-style democracy is poorly equipped to enforce tough love. Election cycles are short and policies that promise immediate benefits are much more attractive than those that entail current sacrifice for the sake of future gain. And human nature is such that it is difficult for us psychologically to own up to our personal failures. When we do make poor decisions that result in poor consequences, it is far too easy for us to conclude our problems are a result of others' actions and not our own. We therefore feel morally justified in asking the government to counterbalance our unluckiness. If the misery makes good television, the camera crews will show up, someone will cry, and the benevolent government will respond.

Yes, I do know this is a terribly callous, easy-to-remember-sounding argument. Of course, some people actually are in bad situations not of their own making and as a society, we will be judged by history partially on the basis of how we treat those individuals. We worry in a practical way about the less fortunate throughout this book. Nevertheless, it would be intellectually dishonest to ignore the hard reality that when we advocate policies that disallow failure, the outcomes of good choices and bad choices become similar. This diminishes the incentives for people to delay immediate gratification and make good choices—one of which is certainly saving money.

As we begin to piece together solutions to America's savings problem, we should be careful not to fall into this trap by proposing public and private policies that provide insurance for those who do not save money. Doing so would surely undercut what we seek to accomplish. People must be allowed to make choices and to live with the consequences of those choices, even if that means they suffer the hardships of living without some of the material possessions we think they should have. It will not work any other way.

Money Is Cheap

Ben Bernanke, chairman of the Federal Reserve Board, has spoken often of the "glut of savings," as if the world taken in totality actually saves *too much* money for its own good.[33] What the chairman really means is that some countries, most notably the governments of some of the larger developing Asian nations, encourage private savings among their citizens and then convert that private savings into U.S. Treasuries.[34] This kind of asset swap artificially inflates the price of U.S. government–backed securities and, by proxy, all dollar-denominated debt. As a direct consequence, this keeps U.S. domestic interest rates lower than they otherwise would be.[35]

This phenomenon relates to U.S. household savings, and the lack of it, in a very direct way. Because these developing nations have an appetite for dollar-denominated debt (bonds), the average American faces savings interest rates that are not particularly attractive. After all, one of the fundamental benefits of saving is earning money on the savings you are essentially lending to someone else. The real interest rates being offered by the market have not been very inspiring for quite some time.[36]

Figure 2.4 displays nominal interest rates, inflation rates, and real interest rates for the period 1975–2005.[37] Real interest rates have not topped 4% since the mid-1980s and in recent years, they have occasionally dipped into negative territory. This is a powerful disincentive to save. If loaning my money to others, even with no substantial risk to my principal, has no positive effect on my future purchasing power, why should I put off consumption until the future?

In a very real way then, the lack of U.S. household savings can be blamed partly on the success of our country. The rest of the world is keenly aware that America's success has bred safe and attractive capital markets. Because dollar-denominated investment instruments are so attractive, they do not have to offer high interest rates. What remains in question is how long this will continue. There are signs that some governments are beginning to move their assets away from dollar-denominated debt. It is too early to tell whether this will result in a large-scale reallocation of government-held wealth or if this is simply the kind of portfolio rebalancing that makes sense to limit governments' exposure to a drop in

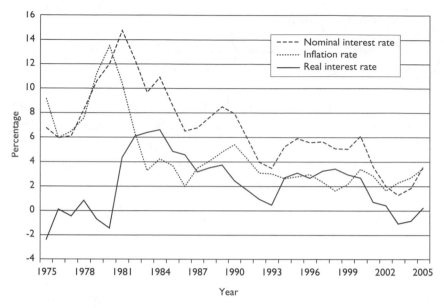

Figure 2.4: Real interest rates, 1975–2005
Source: Author.

the value of the dollar. We have already discussed the problems that would arise if there was a rapid movement of foreign capital out of U.S. markets. But it is equally true that some gradual weakening of foreign demand for dollar-denominated assets would probably nudge real interest rates up in a way that would ultimately prove healthy for the financial well-being of U.S. households, rebalancing the demand for consumption with the desire to save.

Misunderstanding the Value of Compound Interest

Much like the effect of low real interest rates, if you do not understand how interest compounding works, your motivation to save is likely to be substantially diminished. Before we discuss financial literacy in the United States, it is important to recognize that compound interest is one of the truly enticing benefits of savings. If you do not fundamentally understand the magnitude of the benefits, you are much more likely to pass up savings for current consumption. Figure 2.5 illustrates the benefits of beginning savings earlier in life. The graph assumes that you save $300 per month, achieve an 8% return on your portfolio, and retire at age 65. The vertical axis depicts your accumulated wealth at age 65, and the horizontal shows how this wealth will vary depending on what age you begin saving. Also shown is the amount of the final accumulated value that is due to principle, what you actually saved, and how much is due to interest. It demonstrates that when people begin saving earlier, the monies they have available for retirement are driven by the compound interest that is generated. For those who begin saving late in life, this is not the case, and the final accumulated value is much closer to the actual amount saved. Even if you have a reasonable understanding of compound interest, you may be surprised by the magnitude of these numbers, and the difference between early and late savers.

These differences in accumulated values have a large impact on the retirement income that may be derived from a person's savings. As a quick experiment, I took the accumulated values from figure 2.5 and asked,

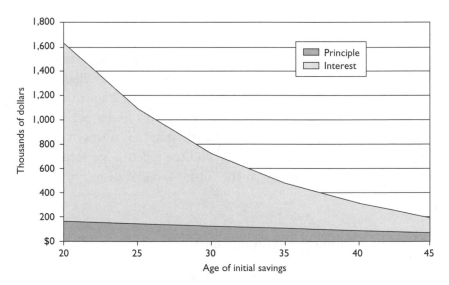

Figure 2.5: The value of compound interest
Source: Author.

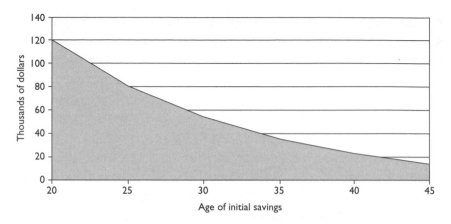

Figure 2.6: Retirement income as a function of the age of initial savings
Source: Author.

"What income can I expect from this retirement savings assuming I only spend my average annual portfolio return (8%) and never touch the principle?"[38] Figure 2.6 shows the results of this simple analysis. Understanding the benefits of consumption is easy; understanding the benefits of compound interest is not.

This misunderstanding is all the more salient in the world of defined-contribution pension plans and online retirement-planning calculators. Particularly for younger workers, the dollar values that pop out of these calculators can seem nothing short of ludicrous: "You are telling me that I need $2.3 million to retire? If that number is right, I am so far in the hole that I don't know where to begin, or even if I *should* begin."[39] The goal seems unattainable. If you do not understand the financial power of compound interest, all may seem lost, and the practical steps that might be taken to improve your lot in the future are lost to the paralysis of hopelessness.

Are We Doing Anything Right?

A natural question to ask at this point, amid all the gloom and doom I've spread liberally throughout this book so far, is: "What, if anything, is right with savings?" Certainly, any solutions we offer should recognize institutional features that have the capability to encourage savings. Mutual funds (a type of investment instrument) and defined-contribution pensions (tax-advantaged retirement accounts) interact with each other in powerful ways to form the backbone of what we might reasonably, if tentatively, call a "success story" in household wealth accumulation. For that reason, these two elements garner a substantial amount of our intellectual attention in the next few chapters. If we can understand what is right and what is wrong in these markets, we will have a solid starting point for making practical recommendations.

To understand the importance of mutual funds, we need to realize the dramatic change they have allowed for savers and investors of low to moderate wealth. They democratized many corners of the financial markets that were previously reserved for wealthy individuals or institutions. They have allowed middle-class households to diversify their assets, and hence reduce their overall risk exposure in ways that were nearly unimaginable a few decades ago.[40] It is very easy to pick up a telephone or use the Internet to invest in funds that specialize in tax-free municipal bonds, real estate investment trusts, high-yield (junk) bonds, gold, equities in the Czech Republic, or just about any other asset class your heart desires. At the level of the average household, mutual funds probably represent the best financial product innovation in the last 50 years.[41] About half of all households in the United States own shares in at least one mutual fund.

What has been even more impressive than the drastically increased prevalence of mutual funds in the investment accounts of American households is their preeminence in the defined-contribution pension market. It is no secret that U.S. companies have been looking for ways to decrease costs associated with their pensions. Many older companies are trying to rid themselves of their legacy of defined-benefit plans. Being financially responsible for the retirement benefits of large numbers of retirees can put enormous strains on a company's balance sheets. General Motors is an outstanding example of a corporation whose pension liabilities have created serious financial problems. These plans require organizations to make actuarially prescribed contributions on behalf of employees in order to yield a specific retirement income that usually is pegged to the employee's compensation and years of service. To combat this problem of sizable annual giving, many employers have moved to defined-contribution pension plans whose costs, while still substantial, are often far less than their defined-benefit counterparts. Under the defined-contribution pension plan, the employer makes predetermined contributions, generally specified as a percentage of the employee's income, to an investment account under the employee's name. The employee can then manage that money however he or she sees fit within the confines of the different investment vehicles offered by the plan. What is nearly ubiquitous in these plans is that the employer contracts with a mutual fund company to offer some of its funds within the plan. Therefore, in addition to alternatives such as company stock and insurance products, many employees now hold shares in mutual funds in their defined-contribution pension plans. Investments in mutual funds currently comprise 22% of the *entire* retirement market in the United States and just more than half of the dollars invested in 401(k) plans, the most popular type of defined-contribution plan.[42]

The way these plans work varies widely. Some employers set up the administrative infrastructure of the plan and contract with a financial services company to provide products in it, but do not make contributions themselves. Employees may contribute if they like, up to limits set by the IRS, but their pension balances will depend only on their own contribution decisions and how they manage their money within the plan. This is a typical setup for many small businesses in the United States. Some employers, often the larger ones, contribute money to the plan for each employee; their contributions may or may not be contingent on employee contributions. An example of a rather standard contingent contribution rule is that the company will match the employee's contributions dollar for dollar up to 5% of his or her base pay. So, if you contribute 2%, the company will kick in 2%, and so forth.

One intuitively appealing aspect of these regular pension contributions is that any money employees decide to contribute is automatically deducted from their paychecks on a pretax basis. That single phrase, "automatically deducted from their paychecks on a pretax basis," points to a number of powerful psychological benefits that we return to later, but it is important to take a cursory look at them here. The word "automatic" is important because it implies that once someone has signed the paperwork, the contributions will continue unless the person does something to stop them. Therefore, in order to continue saving, an employee simply "chooses" the default option, which is to "do nothing." Humans, it turns out, are very good at doing nothing. Marketers are highly aware of this tendency and use it to their advantage when they ask us to purchase products and services. For example, I recently subscribed to the online version of *Consumer Reports* magazine. They quoted me a price for the service and asked me to pay via credit card, which I did. As part of the subscription agreement, it automatically renews each year, and my credit card is charged accordingly, unless I inform them that I want to cancel the subscription. At the time that I subscribed, it was not possible to tell them that I only wanted the subscription to last for one year, so I have to wait for one year and then cancel. We can be quite confident that if *Consumer Reports* asked subscribers to make an active decision to renew their subscriptions each year, their renewal rates would be much lower than they are with this automatic, "do nothing" renewal system. In the world of marketing, there are countless examples of how changing the default option on purchasing a product from active to passive and vice versa dramatically impacts purchase behavior. "Automatic" proves to be a word of importance when discussing savings behavior.

The next part of the phrase, "deducted from their paychecks," is equally important. It makes no financial difference to employees if we deduct an agreed-upon pension contribution from their salary before or after it is given to them, but it makes a large psychological difference. Ask someone why he or she likes to have savings deducted from his or her paycheck and you will likely get some form of this response: "It's like I never really had the money, so I don't miss it." It is far easier for most people to receive a check for $900 than to receive a check for $1,000 and then set aside $100 for savings, even though the net amount in their bank account is the same. The word "deducted" is also a recurring theme in our examination of savings behavior.

Finally, and still embedded in that one short phrase, the word "pretax" takes on special importance. Because most contributions to defined-contribution pension plans are tax deductible, the taxable amount taken from the employee's paycheck is less than the amount that gets deposited into the pension plan. The difference is the income tax on the amount of the contribution, tax that is deferred until the time the money is withdrawn. So when an employee asks his or her payroll office to begin deducting $50 per pay period to contribute to a tax-deferred savings plan, the amount actually deducted is $50 × (1 − employee's marginal tax rate), while the full amount is credited to their tax-deferred account. This difference has the psychological effect of a bonus or rebate, something costing less than it should, which makes us feel better about the decision. For example, this is one of the reasons why automobile manufacturers offer rebates. They could just drop the price by $500, but offering that same amount as a rebate increases our happiness with the transaction. That is also partially why many people plan their income taxes so that they get a refund at the end of the year instead of having to pay, even when it should be clear that what they are doing is effectively lending the federal government money at an interest rate of zero, which makes little financial sense. The financial optimality of the decision is trumped by the pure psychology of receiving a check in the mail.

Given that "automatically deducted from their paychecks on a pretax basis" pushes so many positive psychological buttons, it should not surprise us that account balances in these kinds of plans contain huge stores of wealth for the American worker. Defined-contribution pension plans are therefore doing something right—encouraging savings—and mutual funds are increasingly the investment instrument of choice within these plans. To the extent that we can make defined-contribution plans and mutual funds "better," there will be large advantages for U.S. households.

From Causes to Tricks

The reasons for the decline in American thrift are varied and complex. The silver bullet answer once again eludes us. The solution resides in the psychology of people, some of which is idiosyncratic to the American mind-set and some of which is as old as mankind itself. This basic psychology of imperfect memory, overconfidence, and the illusion of control mixes with the macroeconomic realities of increasing income disparities and low real interest rates to form conditions ripe for what we now see—U.S. households throwing caution to the wind and incurring debt rather than managing savings.

Where do we go from here? We are not yet ready to start laying out the answers. In order to make prescriptions, it is important that we understand not only the psychology and economics of the problem's causes but also how individuals are likely to react given different possible steps toward the solution. We need to understand how people handle what money they do have, the mistakes they make, and the tricks they often play on themselves. We can then turn these cognitive tricks to our collective advantage. We will trick them into saving more money.

Chapter 3 is a narrative about many common financial decision situations that we face in our daily lives and how we make those decisions. In some situations, we make smart decisions; other times, even the best of us make them poorly—sometimes very poorly.

3

THE PSYCHOLOGY OF MONEY

People handle their money in strange ways. Some people make poor financial decisions regularly, and it is clear that those poor decisions can have major negative economic consequences for them. If someone is constantly running up credit card debt, borrowing against home equity to finance vacations, and not contributing to a 401(k) plan, we can say with a fair degree of confidence that this person is not strong in the area of household financial management. Many of us feel a bit smug and self-congratulatory when we think about people like this. After all, we do not fall into those traps. We deal with money carefully and rationally. Or do we?

Let's start this chapter with a hard look at financial literacy among Americans. How well do we really understand the investment options that we confront almost every day? At this point you may be thinking that I'm about to go on a diatribe about how collectively stupid we are, how we don't understand basic math, and how we subsequently make terrible decisions regarding our money. Americans are used to reading newspaper articles offering statistics suggesting that most of us think Zimbabwe is a province in Northern Canada or don't know that World War II came after World War I. Those kinds of articles tend to be more of a rant about the stupidity of the average American rather than being insightful about why we are largely ignorant of the referenced facts or what we should do about it. I promise not to rant in this chapter, but I will provide some scary statistics that point to a widespread misunderstanding of the basics of financial markets. From there I will ask more fundamental questions about the cognitive underpinnings of these errors. Why is financial decision making hard? The answers lead us to a more informed understanding of what to do when asking the final question of the book: What can the public and private sector do to increase household savings?

Financial Literacy

Let's be frank about the thesis of this section: we are collectively not very bright when it comes to basic concepts in finance. In a 2006 study, a nationally representative group of Americans over the age of 50 were asked the following three questions:[1]

1. Suppose you had $100 in a savings account and the interest rate was 2% per year. After five years, how much do you think you would have in the account if you left the money to grow: more than $102, exactly $102, less than $102?
2. Imagine that the interest rate on your savings account was 1% per year and inflation was 2% per year. After one year, would you be able to buy more than, exactly the same as, or less than you can buy today with the money in this account?
3. Do you think that the following statement is true or false? "Buying a single company stock usually provides a safer return than a stock mutual fund."

These questions were devised to test the respondents' basic understanding of compound interest, inflation or real return, and the risk associated with an undiversified portfolio, respectively. It would be difficult to come up with a simpler set of questions to test financial acumen.

How many people responded correctly? Question 1 (compound interest)=67%, Question 2 (inflation)=75%, and Question 3 (stock)=52%. About one-third (34%) of this nationally representative sample answered all three questions correctly. What about issues that are slightly more difficult but closely related to the types of questions that should be considered when devising a retirement savings plan? A survey conducted by John Hancock found that three out of four respondents could not correctly identify the relationship between long-run interest rates and bond prices, and two-thirds were unaware that money market funds do not include stocks.[2] This ignorance regarding the asset holdings of money market funds is particularly salient because many defined-contribution pension plans use money market funds as their default allocation. If the employee does not make an allocation decision, the organization invests 100% of its company-sponsored retirement monies in an account that holds only cash or very short-term debt obligations. The John Hancock study strongly suggests that many people incorrectly believe that leaving all of their retirement funds in a money market account offers them some exposure to equities or broad-based asset allocation.

Beyond the basics of financial markets, people also display a disturbing degree of ignorance about the important institutional features of their employer-sponsored retirement plans. For example, in one study sponsored by the Brookings Institution, the authors compared what a group of respondents within 10 years of retirement thought they knew about their employer-sponsored retirement plans with the administrative records of the relevant plans.[3] Only half of these employees could correctly identify their plan as being either a defined-contribution or defined-benefit plan, and fewer than half knew when they would be eligible for full retirement benefits.

This all adds up to a large proportion of the population that understands neither the full benefits of savings (compound interest question) nor the market and institutional mechanisms for making intelligent choices about how to save. On the other hand, we all understand how to spend. Right now, you can get in your car and drive to a store where you can spend a lot of money very quickly. I am sure that you know how to do this, and you can even name the store at which the money would exit your wallet or purse most rapidly. The benefits of that spending are clear and immediate—a new set of Bose noise-cancelling headphones is waiting to be hooked up to your iPod portable media player, ready to be enjoyed. Spending is easy. Saving is hard. And saving requires some kind of plan.

The Propensity to Plan

Some people just do not plan. We each know a few of these people. They perpetually show up late to everything. They begin packing for a flight about the same time they should be leaving for the airport. They do not pay their bills on time. Their lives seem to move quickly from one crisis to the next. They may be very interesting and warmhearted, but taking actions today to make their lives better down the road is not their forte.

There is increasing evidence that the ability to resist temptation—to forego immediate pleasure in order to stick to a longer-term goal—is a very basic and important trait in predicting life outcomes. This is an important concept in a rapidly expanding area of psychological research known as "emotional intelligence" or "EQ."[4] In the most celebrated of the early EQ experiments, four-year-old children were given one marshmallow each and promised another if they could wait 20 minutes before eating the first one. Some children were able to resist the temptation to eat the marshmallow, while others gobbled it down immediately. The experimenters then tracked the progress of each child participant into adulthood and demonstrated that those with the ability to wait were more successful in life than those who could not, both in terms of careers and interpersonal relationships.[5]

Even the economics literature that focuses the choice behavior of perfectly rational economic agents has concluded that temptation and the inability to delay gratification should be incorporated in models that are trying to predict actual economic behavior.[6] In one particularly salient line of inquiry, researchers were able to cast serious doubt on the long-held belief among many economists that differences in savings rates and wealth accumulation among people with similar socioeconomic backgrounds was primarily due to variations in preferences.[7] They found that differences in preferences for future consumption explained very little of what was happening in the data. Rather, there seemed to be dramatic variances among individuals regarding the "propensity to save," which could not be explained by traditional life-cycle models. These psychological differences loomed large in determining that amount of wealth people accumulated for retirement.

One academic study, conducted in 2003 with the cooperation of the large financial services provider TIAA-CREF (Teachers Insurance and Annuity Association–College Retirement Equities Fund), linked differences in savings rates directly to people's planning behavior in areas of their lives not related to financial planning.[8] It is difficult to determine whether having a financial plan leads to wealth or vice versa. The researchers, therefore, wanted to be careful to uncover general planning behavior to determine whether people who plan a lot for other things in their lives are also more likely to construct a financial plan and, in so doing, increase their financial security in retirement. They asked TIAA-CREF pension plan participants to agree or disagree with statements such as:[9]

- I have spent a great deal of time developing a financial plan.
- Before going on vacation, I spend a great deal of time examining where I would most like to go and what I would like to do.
- I am highly confident in my mathematical skills.

They found that vacation planners also tended to be financial planners and that financial planners did indeed accumulate more wealth. They also found that individuals who self-reported being better at math were more likely to make financial plans regardless of their vacation-planning behavior. The authors concluded that some existing inherent financial propensity to plan is influenced both by the individuals' general attitudes and behavior toward planning (vacation question) as well as their skill set for constructing a reasonable plan (math question). Planners, it seems, end up with more money.

While this research is useful in thinking about the savings problem, part of what is happening here is the time-honored tradition among academics of carefully documenting the obvious.[10] Ask anyone walking down the street and they will undoubtedly express a belief that some people just "have it together" and others do not. Those who have it together make plans, work hard in school, get steady jobs, make money, buy houses and stocks, and retire to warm climates. And some do not.

I think some of this "propensity to plan" is nature, not nurture—some people are just born with more of it than others. We are not suddenly going to make irresponsible people become responsible or make planners out of those who never think ahead. That would be naïve. But that does not mean that we should abandon the issue entirely. If we can make planning easier, at least some people will take advantage of that. If we emphasize the types of skills in our educational curricula that make financial planning possible, we can turn some people toward making better plans.

Nature is stubborn and those who are genetically disposed to impulsivity and not planning for the future will not change much. But I believe there remains a large group of individuals who would like to make financial plans, but lack the basic skills necessary to do so. Teaching those skills will fall not only to our traditional system of education but also to private businesses.

Mental Accounting and Money Management

As it turns out, nearly all of us play tricks on ourselves when it comes to dealing with our own financial situations. We make decisions designed not only to make financial sense but also to make sense of our own feelings of self-worth and intelligence. One example of a self-deceiving trick is the tendency to think in percentages when we are spending large amounts of money, such as shopping for a car or renovating a house. Many of us have purchased a car—the generally dreaded process of nego-tiating a price with the salesperson and the final relief that comes when it has all been settled. The self-deception begins once we have convinced ourselves that spending $25,000 is the right thing to do and we are ready to drive the car home from the showroom. That is when the salesperson is likely to offer several add-ons: "Would you like an extended warranty, some vehicle undercoating, fabric protector on the upholstery, perhaps?" On any other day, spending $150 for fabric protector might seem like a ridiculous idea, but not today. Today you have spent $25,000—what's $150 more? You convince yourself that it is nothing compared with the price of the car, but in reality, that $150 spends (or saves) the same as any other money you might have, regardless of whether you earned it at work or won it in a bowling league. That money could be used for fabric protector today or a couple of new tires a few years from now. Yet today, with the imminent purchase of a new car, we link the added expense to the price of the car; we form a ratio, or percentage, with the money and convince ourselves that $150 is really not that much money in the scheme of things.

A home remodeling project is an even more pernicious example of this behavior. For example, Mike and Mary's home is badly in need of remod-eling, and they must make countless individual decisions about the amount of money they are willing to spend to fix it up. They need a new refrigerator, which can cost anywhere from about $300 to $5,000. How much should they spend? They run into a type of cognitive double whammy in this situation. It is easy to compare the price of the refrigerator to the entire cost of the renovation project and conclude that just about any price is relatively insignificant. But the problem doesn't stop there. Because there are so many refrigerators at different price levels, it is easy for our couple to compare the cost of each more-expensive model with the one priced just below it and conclude, "Well, it is only $50 more for the extra-large crisper." Once they have satisfied themselves that the deluxe crisper is indeed worth the relatively paltry amount of extra cash, they move on to consider the model priced just above that, and so forth. For each individual purchase decision, they end up spending somewhat more than they had originally anticipated. A remodeling project budgeted to cost $30,000 therefore ends up costing them twice that much, and each individual decision was perfectly justifiable in their minds.

This cognitive self-deception—the propensity to form ratios with money in order to make ourselves believe that spending is relatively insignificant—directly applies to the way many financial services are currently priced in the marketplace. Which sounds more expensive, $1,000 or 1.2%? Of course, this is in some ways a nonsensical question—you need to know 1.2% of *what*. But, just at the pure gut level, $1,000 looks pretty big and 1.2% looks pretty small. If, however, you have $250,000 invested in your 401(k) plan and 1.2% is your average annual expense ratio of the funds in which the money is invested, then that 1.2% is costing you about three times what a flat $1,000 annual fee would cost you. Mutual fund fees are quoted in small percentages for a reason: people's natural psychological tendency is to equate small ratios with "not that much money." It is the car salesman in different clothing.

Richard Thaler has thought extensively about the tricks people play on themselves to rationalize their spending and savings behavior. The example above is a consequence of what Thaler calls "mental accounting," and the broader implications of that theory of human financial behavior are enormous.[11] At its most primitive level, the theory of mental accounting posits that the way we think about any given sum of money is transaction-specific; a dollar earned from hard work will be treated differently than a dollar won at the racetrack. A marginal dollar spent in conjunction with a larger purchase will be considered differently than a dollar purchase on its own. Such thoughts violate what economists typically call the "fungibility" assumption—the idea that money is perfectly fungible, or interchangeable, across different types of transactions, and hence all dollars should be treated the same. A dollar is a dollar. Others have extended the basic architecture of the theory to examine phenomena such as how people mentally code savings and debt decisions[12] and how consumers react to price discounts and sales at retail outlets.[13]

Let us dig into this theory of human behavior a bit more, to flesh out its implications as it relates to savings and consumption. Some examples inspired by Thaler's original mental accounting paper are a good place to start.[14] In each of the following decision situations, ask yourself which alternative you would feel better about. There are no right or wrong answers. Each situation presents you with two alternatives that are intended to be financially equivalent. Do not overthink it. There are no strange tax implications or other complicated economic phenomena at play; this is just a simple evaluation of which situation would make you happier. Consider the following two scenarios:

1. Maria finds a $10 bill lying in the gutter.
2. David finds a $20 bill lying in the gutter. Shortly after finding the money, he learns that he has been issued a $10 fine for a parking meter violation.

Who is happier, Maria or David? Let's try one more.

1. Maria receives a check for $8,000, profit from an investment she had previously made. Later that day, she receives notice from the company that advised her to make the investment that their fee for advising her is $500. She writes out a check to the investment advisor and mails it.
2. David receives a check for $7,500, the net profit from an investment he had previously made.

Who is happier, Maria or David?

If your answers follow what is typical for these types of questions, you answered that Maria is happier in the first scenario and David is happier in the second. Why is it possible for most people to agree on this, given that the financial situations are completely equivalent? What's going on here?

Both scenarios point to that same underlying psychological phenomenon. The pain of losing $X outweighs the pleasure of receiving $X. If we want to apply standard economic terminology, our utility function for losses is more sensitive to a given dollar amount than our utility function for gains. Or for poets, it is better never to have loved than to have loved and lost.

In our first scenario, both characters end up with $10. But David starts with an additional $10 in his hand; it is his, he owns it. To give up $10 of his $20 is more painful than if he never had the extra $10 in the first place. Maria has no such complicated angst; she simply receives a nice $10 bonus.

In the second scenario, Maria must go through the psychologically painful process of writing a check to her investment advisor. Maria's net return is exactly the same as David's, but David never explicitly sees any fees and, moreover, he does not have to write a check to pay anyone. At the end of the day, he is a bit happier than Maria.

We make efforts to construct our financial lives in ways that make us happier. For instance, we might believe that it is better to have federal taxes taken out of our regular paychecks than to face a large tax bill at the end of the year. However, from a strict financial standpoint, it may make sense to owe some amount of money at the end of the year rather than give the government what is actually a zero-interest loan. Even if the reality is that we receive a somewhat smaller paycheck and lose some money on the transaction—foregone interest—many of us do it because it makes us feel happier.

Because of this transaction-specific utility, we also implicitly understand that it is far easier to save a dollar we have never held in our hand than it is to save one we have taken possession of and feel that we own. By extension, it is also psychologically less painful to get a regular paycheck in the amount of $(X-Y)$ than it is to get one for $X and then turn around and write a check for $Y to your retirement savings account. Therefore, even though from a purely rational decision-making standpoint it may make sense to save a little less money this month and a little more next month, that is not the way successful savers behave. Regular, automatic, fixed-amount deductions from a paycheck ease the pain.

This theory, perhaps more than any other theory of human behavior besides canonical economics, proves useful in devising some practical ways to make the decision to save more attractive. Let's continue for the moment, however, to explore the ways in which individuals systematically make poor financial decisions.

I Am Smarter than You

Most people think they are smarter than average. They think they know more than they do, and they are more confident in that knowledge than they should be.[15] Men are more prone to it than women, but most individuals overestimate their abilities. Authors have speculated about why that is the case; conventional wisdom holds that unrealistic views of one's abilities may have had some survival advantage for early mankind. For instance, an early hunter, out looking for rabbits, might inadvertently stumble upon a mountain lion. If the hunter acted weak and cowardly, the mountain lion would have a quick breakfast. If, on the other hand, the hunter could convince the mountain lion that he would be a tough fight, a rather unrealistic prospect, the mountain lion might move on to find weaker prey. This conjecture closely follows modern-day advice of what to do if you meet a mountain lion—act like a tough guy! Nevertheless, evolutionary biologists—who study the primitive causes of those types of persistent psychological phenomena—call some of these kinds of naturally hardwired thoughts "maladaptive."[16] In short, maladaptive behaviors are those that would have been beneficial to the survival of early humans but are detrimental to good decision making in the modern state of humankind. For example, early humans learned to like sugar because it signaled high caloric content, which was a beneficial attribute when food was scarce and starving to death was a real threat. Most people still find foods with high sugar content to be tasty, even though, particularly in developed countries, death due to obesity is more likely than death due to starvation.

Meetings with mountain lions are less likely to happen these days than meetings with financial advisors, and our evolutionary propensity to magnify our capabilities may doom us in our encounters with the financial marketplace. Shefrin notes two main implications for overconfidence in the financial marketplace: "The first is that investors take bad bets because they fail to realize that they are at an informational disadvantage. The second is that they trade more frequently than is prudent, which leads to excessive trading volume."[17] Put simply, overconfident individuals think they can beat the market. Whether anyone can beat the market over the long term is a question that inspires passionate debate. We do not need to wade into those arguments to come to the nearly tautological conclusion that the average investor cannot beat the market. The average overconfident investor trades on these delusional beliefs and consequently accumulates the costs associated with trading. Active traders' brokerage fees, bid–ask spreads,[18] and taxes can substantially erode any investment gains they have accrued, leaving them with a net return lower than their nonactive trader counterparts. That is the essence of Brad Barber and Terrance Odean's finding that individual investors who trade the most make the least, and those most prone to self-detrimental active trading are overconfident men.[19]

Overconfidence also has a more subtle but perhaps even more powerful effect than encouraging active trading. Consider this line of thinking: "I have a very optimistic view of my own future. Given that I am so smart and generally above average, I expect to make a higher income in the future and hence spend more of my income today. Therefore, I'm less likely to save." If this were not the case, taking on debt to fund income-increasing education would never be a reasonable decision. We need to deal with this misrepresentation of the facts if we want to devise savings strategies that can make a difference.

Fooled by Randomness

Carl Sagan once speculated about why many of us see the image of a face when we look at the full moon on a clear night.[20] He argued that babies learn quickly to recognize a human face if they want attention and the food that comes with it. Even when their vision is still highly undeveloped and their sight blurry, babies who can discern a face and smile back at their caregivers get more attention, and are more likely to survive, than those who do not. A cute grin yields food, and in the long sweep of human history, much like our story of the hunter and the mountain lion, nature favors those who get food rather than become food. Because of the immediate benefit of recognizing a face, another important cognitive phenomenon has evolved. If any random pattern of clouds, rocks, or potato chips even slightly resembles a face, our minds will organize that information so that it does. Our brains are telling us, "It is better to wrongly see a face than to wrongly miss a face and risk not getting fed and protected." And so we look up at the full moon on a clear night and from the random craters and shadows emerges the face of a somewhat odd-looking old man.

Recognizing faces is one outstanding example of the natural human tendency to find patterns in anything. Our minds find patterns and meaning in the obscure. Below, I have listed the results of flipping a coin 20 times, where "H" indicates "heads" and "T" indicates "tails."[21]

T T H T T H H H H H H T T T T H T H H H

Now consider the sequence below. It is the result of asking my wife to give me a random sequence of "heads" and "tails," as if a coin were being tossed 20 times:

H H T H T T T H H T T H H T T H H T H T

Notice the difference between the actual and the imagined sequences. The actual sequence will look to most people like something less than random. With that long string of Hs, it does not look haphazard enough to be believable. But, of course, nothing fishy is going on at all. In fact, a longish-looking string of Hs or Ts is likely to show up in a sequence of 20 coin tosses. The sequence my wife came up with looks more random to us, because it contains more alternating outcomes and no consecutive streaks. In our minds, streaks imply meaning and cause, while lack of streaks implies randomness.

A classic study of the human tendency to look for and find patterns in random events involved the analysis of basketball players shooting free throws.[22] This skill varies, but many casual and even some avid observers of the sport believe that individual players go through shooting "streaks" in which the probability that they will make a free throw departs markedly from their average propensity to sink them. Players can be on a "hot" or "cold" streak depending on how they have been hitting them lately. Implicit in this belief is that on any given free throw, the probability that a player will sink it depends not only on his or her long-run average but also on what kind of streak he or she happens to be having at the moment. To the believer in streaks, the underlying probabilities have changed.

Much like our coin toss example, though, the evidence strongly suggests that basketball players' free throw–shooting skills really do not go through streaks. If J. J. Redick's free throw–shooting average is 90%, the probability of his sinking it on any given free throw should be 90%.[23] Whether he hit or missed his last five throws is irrelevant for prediction purposes. Tell that to many basketball fans, however, and they will never believe you because they infer meaning from the strings of hits and misses.

How one views the probabilities of basketball free throws is probably not terribly important to public policy, but it is important how people view past financial events. There is a whole industry built around using the past performance of mutual funds to rate their worthiness as investments. The most pervasive of these is Morningstar's star-rating system, in which past performance information is combined with other fund characteristics to rate funds on a one- to five-star scale. However, the bulk of evidence about the mutual fund market strongly suggests that past performance is a miserable predictor of future performance. Many studies of this market find that there is absolutely no predictive value whatsoever in the past performance numbers.[24] That puts our coin toss and basketball examples in a much more serious context. Yet, the market for financial information continues to pump out past-performance rankings and corresponding advice because our pattern- and meaning-seeking minds cannot help but believe there is something of value there. We buy it.

Simplifying Heuristics in the Face of Complex Financial Problems

Saving a sufficient amount of money for retirement is an exceedingly difficult task for many people, even those who believe they are much smarter than average. It is also the subject of an abundance of books, magazine articles, seminars, and radio shows. The topic stresses out a lot of people, and the media and professional financial planners capitalize on that stress. Why is it such a problem? At the most fundamental level, there are two reasons why saving for retirement is difficult. First, for the bulk of our earning years, retirement seems a long way off. It is difficult to give up that nice new watch today for the possibility of having a little more money 20 years from now. What I can purchase with the money today is very real to me, what psychologists sometimes call "vivid," while the allure of some distant future consumption is faint.

Second, the problem of how much to save is complicated and requires knowledge of all kinds of future contingencies that are difficult to predict. It is such a burdensome problem that a 2006 survey conducted by the Employee Benefit Research Institute (EBRI) found that only 42% of workers had ever tried to determine how much money they will need for retirement.[25] A Brookings Institution study found that fewer than half of all workers within 10 years of retirement could correctly identify their employer's retirement plan as a defined-contribution or defined-benefit plan, and fewer than half could correctly state the year in which they would become eligible for retirement benefits.[26]

Economists have developed elaborate models, generally called life-cycle models, which offer prescriptions about how households should save to allow for sufficient consumption in retirement. No one I know would seriously argue that households solve those models to determine appropriate savings. That fact, in and of itself, however, does not condemn the models. To catch a Frisbee, a dog does not need to solve the complicated mathematical equation that describes its flight. But a complicated mathematical expression can provide an excellent description of where the dog will run to catch it. If we are simply interested in predicting behavior rather than describing the thought process that leads to it, sometimes doing some math will suffice.

Back in the world of modeling human behavior, to actually solve a life-cycle model of savings, it is necessary for an individual to make educated guesses about, among other things, how long he or she will live and what the expected rate of return will be on his or her portfolio over the next 30 years or so. Although we may have some useful knowledge about those variables, the uncertainty with which we make educated guesses renders the formal decision problem very complex.[27] Even among economists, there is a growing consensus that, absent some "exotic" preferences, those models do a poor job—not only in describing the decision process, which is obvious, but also in predicting behavior.[28] Math seems to be able to handle the dog with the Frisbee, but not individual savings decisions.

A growing body of evidence shows that psychological and other institutional factors not included in these models play a significant role in retirement savings behavior and that the traditional models do not even come close to what the average household is doing. Real households, as opposed to idealized households, develop simple and sometimes simplistic rules of thumb for dealing with otherwise very complex decision problems. Part of the reason is probably that they cannot do the math, but some of it also undoubtedly stems from the fact that individuals seek to solve problems that preserve their feelings of confidence and intelligence. The last thing I want to do is try to solve a problem that leaves me feeling like an idiot. That contradicts what I believe I know about myself in some very painful ways. It is better to reengineer the problem into something that I can actually solve. I may or may not realize it is a bit of a simplification, but I did solve the problem and therefore I sleep better at night. There are some patterns to the ways people simplify complex decision problems. We now turn to some of those rules of thumb.

Freedom from Choice

We live in a world that worships freedom of choice. More choice is considered necessarily better because we can always reject alternatives that do not interest us. Freedom to choose implies a greater capacity for self-expression and actualization. A shoe store that carries more shoes is better than one that carries fewer. More options for media, ice cream, and car models are assumed to make us happier.[29]

Perhaps the most elegantly articulated arguments for the moral and economic superiority of individual choice across a wide range of personal and political contexts are Milton Friedman's classic books, *Capitalism and Freedom* and *Free to Choose*. They are intellectually powerful and offer compelling arguments against government restrictions on individual choice. What if, on the other hand, there are some situations in which people strongly desire to have their choices limited and would be demonstrably better off for it?

Marketers have understood this concept for a long time; offering consumers more choice does not always make them happier. It is common knowledge in product marketing that when faced with a situation in which there are too many choices, consumers will develop rules of thumb that ignore much of the product information available to them.[30] They become overwhelmed, and simple choice heuristics help ameliorate that feeling. To get some sense of that effect, consider the last time you wanted to paint a room in your house or apartment. Before the painting process began, you visited your local hardware store or home center and collected information, probably in the form of small paint chips or color sample cards. Depending on your personality type, that may have been a daunting task— who knew there could be so many shades of *white*? If there were only 20 colors available, you probably would have immediately eliminated the 15 or so that were obviously out of the question and focused your attention on choosing one of the few remaining color options in a reasonably short amount of time. But there were more like 2,000 colors, and the information overload may have caused you to procrastinate. Ultimately, you may have made a choice, but were you genuinely happier than you would have been had the choice set only contained 20 paint colors? In the latter case, perhaps you could have found a paint you liked *and* had the time to mow the lawn or watch a movie instead of agonizing over your large stack of paint chips.

In one study, Sheena Iyengar, a social psychologist on the business faculty at Columbia University, devised a set of experiments that included presenting customers in a high-end grocery store with different assortments of "exotic jams" that they could sample from a tasting booth. The jams were all variants of the same brand, Wilkin & Sons. Some customers saw an assortment of 24 jams, while others saw just six. The results were striking. Although more of the customers were initially enticed by the larger selection of jams, a much greater percentage of the people who viewed the smaller selection actually made a purchase. A full 30% of those who saw the more modest selection purchased the jam, while only 3% of the others did. It appears that the customers' motivation to buy was hampered by too much choice.[31]

As it turns out, this type of information overload and subsequent choice deterrence happens not only with paint and exotic jams but also with investment products. A shockingly large proportion of people chose not to choose when faced with the decision of how to allocate their retirement monies in their employer-sponsored tax-deferred savings plan, letting a valuable opportunity fly by. The problem is significantly worse in situations where employees are making decisions in the context of an employer-sponsored plan with many options.[32] For many people, that type of asset-allocation decision is difficult and intimidating. Faced with many options, they become overwhelmed and choose to do nothing. The problem with deciding not to decide in this situation is that the default option of most plans is to place 100% of the employer contribution in a money market account, which invests solely in very-short-term debt obligations. While there is nothing inherently wrong with holding some money in a money market account, the long-run expected return on such accounts is often lower than the expected rate of inflation. For the vast majority of employees, therefore, holding all of their retirement assets in a money market account is a miserable investment strategy; it is an asset allocation that virtually guarantees a poor rate of return.

These difficult choice scenarios also lead to other types of self-defeating behavior. In the face of these choices, investors have a propensity to develop simplistic diversification heuristics instead of ones that make better financial sense. For example, given a 401(k) plan with some number N mutual funds to choose from, a disturbingly large percentage of people will place $1/N$ of their money in each mutual fund regardless of the underlying assets in which the fund invests. These investors try to diversify over mutual funds, treating mutual funds as assets in and of themselves, instead of diversifying their actual asset holdings. If a company's plan has more bond funds, the employees end up with an asset allocation heavy in bonds. If the plan contains mostly equity funds, their retirement holdings skew toward equities. Shlomo Bernartzi and Richard Thaler found evidence of this kind of naïve diversification strategy when examining the retirement allocation choices of state employees in Arizona and California.[33] Because the mutual funds contained in those states' retirement plans are quite different—one contains a high proportion of bond mutual funds while the other offers more stock mutual funds—Bernartzi and Thaler determined that many of the employees had asset-allocation strategies that were invariant to the investment strategies of the funds held within the plan. Many were following the $1/N$ diversification heuristic with no regard for asset holdings of the mutual funds contained in the plan. In other words, they were trying to follow the age-old investment advice of not putting all of their eggs in one basket, but they really did not understand what "basket" meant in this context. Therefore, some investors were unwittingly concentrating their retirement savings in one particular asset class and consequently were taking on far more risk than they understood. In the present world of defined-contribution pension plans, this naïve approach to diversification is a serious problem.

In some cases of substantial financial consequence, therefore, more choices lead to bad decision making. Poor decision making in this situation means investing your savings in ways that can increase risk, reduce potential growth, or both—neither of which is a particularly good idea. Overcoming this cognitive bias will involve proactive U.S. employers. By properly structuring their defined-contribution pension plans, employers can reduce these pervasive errors.

Anchoring and Adjusting

Often the hardest part of making a complex decision is how to start thinking about the problem. Our minds search for a starting point from which other observable information can be added to arrive at a final conclusion. Starting points can be pieces of data related to the problem at hand, but also can be conscious or subconscious preconceptions about the way the world works. For example, I have very little idea of how long it will take to paint the fence and the pergola in my backyard. But the last time I painted a fence, it took about two long days. My current fence is a little more involved than the last one because it has multiple gates with surrounding trim, and I want to coat it with a water sealer before I start painting. Using my prior experience of two days as a starting point, I estimate that this project is likely to take four days. Psychologists would say that I am "anchoring" on my initial experience of two days and "updating" based on some other information I know about the project. We'll see if my four-day estimation turns out to be correct.

It would be nice if these starting points, or "anchors," were always as neat, tidy, and rational as the one presented here. Unfortunately, anchors can be utterly arbitrary. In a famous experiment conducted by Nobel laureate Daniel Kahneman and Amos Tversky, a group of students were asked to estimate the percentage of United Nations member states that were African.[34] Before eliciting an exact percentage, each student took one spin on a *Wheel of Fortune*–type wheel that contained the numbers between 1 and 100. The participants were initially asked whether they believed the percentage of African countries in the United Nations was above or below the number they got on their spin of the wheel. For example, a participant who spun the number 70 was asked whether he or she believed that the actual percentage was greater than or less than 70. Subsequently, the students were asked to provide their best estimate. Remember that the participants were fully aware that the number assigned to them was randomly generated from a spin of the wheel. A perfectly rational decision maker should have inferred absolutely no information from the number he or she was presented. However, that is not what occurred. Students who spun the number 10 gave an average estimate of 25%. For those whom fate assigned the number 65, the average estimate was 45%. The wheel spin mattered, even though it is hard to argue that it should have.

This kind of arbitrary anchoring experiment has been replicated many times since its original incarnation. Many of these experiments have been published, but countless others have not. One of my colleagues at Darden attended a seminar given by Daniel Kahneman in which he asked the audience—mostly academics who would have been well aware of his anchoring experiments—to write down the last four digits of their Social Security numbers. He then asked them to estimate the number of physicians in the state where the seminar was being held. Sure enough, there was a strong positive correlation between the last four digits of the respondents' Social Security numbers and their estimates of the number of physicians.[35] The mind works in strange and interesting ways.

I have also done some of this casual experimentation, just to convince myself that the results are true. In a course I taught with my finance colleague, Michael Schill, I split the class into three groups and via an online survey queried them about their expectations for inflation. Students were first asked whether they believed that over the next 12 months inflation would be above or below X, where X took on the value randomly assigned to students as either 3%, 4.5%, or 6%. They were then asked what they believed the inflation rate would be over the next 12 months. Sure enough, there was a positive correlation between the assigned random anchor and the elicited inflation estimate. It is now accepted wisdom among social psychologists and decision scientists that these effects, however mysterious, are indeed true and powerful.[36]

The world provides us with anchors every day; these are the points of reference we use to make judgments. Some anchors are physical. For instance, because I am sitting in a chair writing at the moment, the probability that I will be in or near this chair in an hour's time is greater than the probability that I will be at the beach. The more interesting anchors, however, are the psychological ones that creep into our thought processes. It is easier for me to decide whether I will work a little more or a little less than usual today than it is for me to do a complete review of my work plans every morning. It is easier for me to have lunch today at the same place as yesterday rather than carefully evaluating all of the choices I have at my disposal. A 70-degree day in March seems warm, while in August it seems cool. For almost any problem or evaluative judgment that our minds grapple with, we first recall the familiar before considering alternatives. If we are pleased with the familiar, we often go with it.

Anchors are enormously important in consumption and savings decisions as well. What kind of house should we buy? What kind of car should we drive? Where should we send our children to school? Even beyond the particulars of consumption and savings rates, anchors can also affect *how* we save. For example, if everyone you know owns some stock, or at least tells you they do, then owning stock seems very normal and you are more likely to invest in some yourself. If your employer matches dollar-for-dollar contributions to the company's 401(k) plan up to a limit of 3% of your gross income, then 3% + 3% = 6% is probably a pretty good number to think about saving for retirement. Although you have never actually calculated how much you will need to save for retirement, you assume your employer picked 6% for a reason, and moving too far from that figure is probably not necessary. You're not quite sure how the money is invested in the company's plan; you never went through that pile of paperwork they handed you about each of the different mutual funds you could select. You know that if you don't make a choice, they will pick a fund for you. Maybe it is not the best fund, but it is probably about as good as you could do picking things on your own. One of these days, you will probably go through that legal stuff to see if you should change anything.

Given our busy lives, this propensity to anchor means that whatever is right in front of us, what we hear about every day, and what others (our employers, for example) do to encourage or discourage certain types of savings have an enormous impact on how we ultimately solve the difficult cognitive problem of how much to save and invest. If our aim is to devise public and private policies that will help increase savings, we had better keep our eye squarely on how individuals are likely to form their anchors and, to the extent possible, devise decision contexts that encourage anchors that generate constructive savings behavior.

Stupidity Aversion

If a short-term U.S. government bond paid a very safe 4% return and the expected return on the stock market was also 4%, almost no one would invest in stocks. Why would you take the risk associated with equity ownership when you could get the same expected return on an asset that would pay with near certainty? This is almost a nonsensical question because if a riskier asset could not provide a superior expected rate of return, the market for that asset would very likely not even exist. The balance between risk and return is a concept that is absolutely fundamental to financial markets. Investors would like to have high return and low risk, and those to whom we are effectively lending money (by investing) would like to offer investors high risk and low return. Practically speaking, the world works out very neatly somewhere in between the desires of the market participants. This is what financial economists call an "efficient frontier," or a trade-off between risk and return that marketable financial assets stick to pretty closely. Large deviations from this frontier are rare, and some would even argue they are nonexistent.

Markets behave this way, but we often do this kind of risk-and-return analysis at the individual level in ways that seem rather strange.[37] In the financial world, individuals make personal judgments about risk and return, deviating in many ways from purely rational economic decision making in their evaluations. Two of these deviations are discussed below because they are important in the recommendations that follow.

First, we do not like feeling stupid. We wish to preserve favorable impressions of ourselves. There are many situations and outcomes in financial markets that have the potential to leave us feeling stupid, and we try to avoid them. We do this by staying away from financial situations that have even the tiniest probability of an unfavorable outcome. In a famous example, the Nobel laureate economist Maurice Allais presented people with two hypothetical alternatives:[38]

Alternative A: Receive $1 million with certainty.
Alternative B: Receive $2.5 million with a probability of 10%, $1 million with a probability of 89%, and nothing with a probability of 1%.

Which one would you choose? Most people choose Alternative A, the $1 million with certainty. There is nothing particularly irrational about that choice, but it does require a very high degree of risk aversion in order to make sense. After all, there is an 89% chance that Alternative B will yield the same financial result as Alternative A ($1 million) and receiving an additional $1.5 million is exactly 10 times more likely than your chances of receiving nothing. You are really playing it safe if you choose Alternative A.

Through other experiments, Allais showed that peoples' choices were not motivated by risk aversion. Many people have speculated about this, most notably the mathematician Leonard Savage.[39] His analysis led to the idea of a psychological phenomenon called "regret aversion." This is the basic idea that people choose Alternative A because they cannot bear the possibility that they may have had $1 million right in their hands but instead essentially gambled it away. They would feel stupid. Even if the gamble itself was utterly rational—for instance, changing the 1% probability of receiving nothing to something even more miniscule like 0.001%—the psychological pain associated with knowing that you gambled away a sure $1 million is just so painfully unthinkable that it is ruled out no matter what potentially higher payoffs might be offered or how small the probability that you will receive nothing. At the level of the individual, economic analysis of risk and return yields to deep-seated psychology.

A second example of where we go wrong can be illustrated by the following scenario, constructed from an idea known as the Ellsberg paradox.[40] Suppose you had a jar containing 90 colored marbles. Thirty of the marbles are blue, and 60 of them are red or black, but you do not know in what proportions (assume the jar is opaque and therefore you cannot make an educated guess about which color is better represented). It could be 50 red and 10 black, vice versa, or any other combination. Which of the following two gambles would you prefer?

Gamble 1: You get $100 if a blue ball is drawn and nothing otherwise.
Gamble 2: You get $100 if a red ball is drawn and nothing otherwise.

Which is the better gamble? From a straight statistical point of view, neither one is better. Your best guess at the number of red balls should be 30, halfway between zero and 60. It may be more or it may be less, but if you are trying to figure how much money you might expect to make from Gamble 2 then your best guess at the probability of winning the $100 should be 30/90 or about 33%. This is, of course, the exact same probability of the payoff in Gamble 1.

Most people, however, strongly prefer Gamble 1. Assuming you picked it too, a reasonable question to ask yourself is, "Why?" The answer lies in the fact that the probabilities in the first gamble are known, while the probabilities in the second gamble are unknown. Most of us tend to feel more comfortable with risky situations in which the probabilities of various outcomes are reasonably well known to us, but less comfortable in situations in which the risks are seemingly more ambiguous. We tend to avoid ambiguous situations, sometimes taking added risk to gain some certainty about the probability of the outcome.

I think the underlying motivations in both illustrations—to avoid feeling stupid for taking a gamble you might regret or for gambling when you do not know the probabilities—have profound implications for how we save our money. Perhaps the most important real-world example of the desire for stupidity avoidance shows up in the broad lack of participation of U.S. households in equity markets. The stock market presents households with an ambiguous risk. For example, if you invested and held money in the stock market for 10 years at any time during the last 50 years, what is the probability that you would have made a positive return? You don't really know, do you? Neither did I, until I calculated it; the answer is about 93%.[41] The probability itself is not as important as the fact that you and I did not know it. What is the probability that you will get your money back plus some return from the certificate of deposit you may have invested in at your bank? We both know the answer to this question, without even calculating it. For all practical purposes, the probability is 100%. Banks do not go belly-up that often and, moreover, up to $100,000 is insured by the federal government. In the world of investing, this is about as unambiguous as it gets. This is also the case for U.S. government bonds that are held to maturity. The probability of a very bad outcome is just about zero (Allais paradox) and there is little ambiguity (Ellsberg paradox). This makes bank instruments and bonds more attractive savings options for many households than suggested by a strict analysis of the financial risks and rewards. It also makes the stock market less attractive.

It is particularly important to note that households with less financial savvy, often the poorer households, are even more likely than most to view stock market returns as ambiguous, an opaque and frightening unknown.[42] This psychological hurdle, and the cycle of poverty that flows from it, will require bold action to overcome.

Turning Irrationality in Our Favor

The irrational and counterintuitive ways that people deal with their money have been of interest to academics for decades. Experiments like the Ellsberg and Allais paradoxes provide tantalizing evidence that there is far more than canonical economics at play when individuals make economic and financial choices. But academic interest is not enough. Rather than remaining naïvely in the world of the perfectly rational saver and investor, we ultimately need to turn our knowledge of human behavior into informed, actionable policies.

This is where we head next, starting with the government because sound policies there can pave the way for enlightened private-sector solutions as well.

4

PUBLIC POLICIES THAT WILL
INCREASE SAVINGS

The kind of man who wants the government to adopt and enforce his ideas
is always the kind of man whose ideas are idiotic.
—H. L. Mencken, "The Divine Afflatus" (1917)

Much can be done to increase household savings in the United
States. The capacity for practical ideas to address this problem resides in
many corners of the federal government, academia, and private enterprise.
Some ideas are grand, such as changing the entire federal tax structure.
Some are more mundane, like changing the default asset allocations
of pension plans. But ameliorating this endemic social problem will require
a series of steps that are large and small—not just one bold gesture.

It would be nice to believe that to solve this problem we only need to
educate people about the importance of saving. Perhaps we should publish
more books and articles that explain the common psychological mistakes
people make when handling their money, and what they could do differently. I am sure it would help. Yet, despite new efforts to distribute information on savings and the good work of groups such as the American
Savings Education Council and Choose to Save, people retain the same
biases and make the same mistakes that they always have. Therefore, the
specific prescriptions detailed below do not assume any intensive educational campaign with the attendant increase in financial knowledge. They
assume that we all come as we are.

Government action can increase the personal savings rate. The state
can and does force most people who are employed to save a certain

amount. It can also provide incentives to save. This has traditionally been accomplished by reducing the tax burden on monies contributed to eligible savings plans. In a more limited sense, businesses can also coerce or offer incentives for personal savings.

Most Americans are forced to spend a specified fraction of their income to purchase a government retirement annuity. These compulsory Social Security contributions are not traditionally considered savings because participants exercise so little control over how the funds are invested and how the proceeds are disbursed. Nevertheless, Social Security does function as a type of forced savings plan. Likewise, many companies offer defined-benefit or defined-contribution retirement plans. Particularly in the case of defined-contribution plans, employees often have some control over the monies, both in terms of their asset allocation and through a limited ability to borrow against those funds prior to retirement. Yet, because those same monies could be given to employees in the form of wages, they act as a forced savings plan.

There are many government-sponsored incentives to save. Most prominent of these incentives allow taxes to be deferred on contributions to retirement accounts. Although tax-deferred retirement accounts have met with some success, these tax incentives have done less than anticipated to spur additional retirement savings, particularly among lower-income groups. In addition to retirement incentives, there are also federal tax breaks available to those who save for medical expenses and state-specific plans that provide tax relief for those who save for higher education.

Beyond those targeted plans, whose main economic impact is retirement savings, it is nearly impossible to force individual Americans to save more money. Our collective political instincts are decidedly libertarian when we consider coercive means to increase the personal savings rate. The basic social values of most Americans, regardless of their political leanings, are not congruent with models such as Singapore's Central Provident Fund (where workers are compelled to save large amounts of their income that can be used for qualified purchases such as homes and education). Coercive measures could raise personal savings rates, but that is not the reality of American politics; indeed, there are completely non-coercive ways to increase personal savings.

Raising aggregate personal savings requires at least one of the following three occurrences. The first, and by far the most obvious, is an increase in the personal savings rate. If people save more of their income, personal savings will increase. Of course, the devil is in the details of how this can be accomplished, and increasing the personal savings rate is only one part of the equation. Second, people can choose to invest their savings in assets that tend to have higher rates of return over time than in instruments with modest or even negative returns. While the macroeconomic environment controls the ultimate return of many investment instruments, we can make reasonable inferences about differences in the expected returns of various asset classes, particularly over extended periods of time. Third, taxes and fees levied by financial services firms subtract from gross savings. The magnitude of those taxes and fees is a far more powerful determinant of the stock of household savings than is generally understood.

Described below is a series of public policy measures that, if implemented, would very likely increase savings. These recommendations range from sweeping changes to the U.S. tax code to modest proposals that call for slightly revised marketing of some government-backed securities. While some ideas are currently tied more closely to one political party or the other, none involve the types of basic value judgments that are intrinsic to a particular political philosophy.

Tax Consumption rather than Income

Our tax system suffers greatly from the tyranny of the status quo; it is a prime example of a pure anchoring effect in the public policy arena. Any proposed change is immediately seen through partisan political lenses. All political punditry, cries of outrage, editorializing in the *New York Times*, and other shrill public comments center on what demographic a particular proposal might benefit relative to the current system. It is sad that the more fundamental question—whether or not the entire structure of the federal income tax system constitutes good public policy—has been relegated to the fringe of public debate. The increasing and persistent imbalance between household consumption and savings provides a powerful argument in favor of doing a de novo review of our federal tax system.

Although the idea of a federal consumption tax rather than a federal income tax is perpetual fodder for conservative talk radio, it is an idea that has enjoyed support across the political spectrum.[1] It has been endorsed by Nobel laureate economists Milton Friedman (conservative) and Kenneth Arrow (liberal), and a long list of other economists with diverse political views. Economists who study the impact and implications of various forms of taxation have generally found strong support for the idea that, relative to taxes on labor income and capital, consumption taxes increase social welfare.[2] Some social commentators have advanced it as a way to save ourselves from destructive overconsumption.[3] In 1995, a bipartisan group of U.S. senators—Pete Domenici (R-NM), Bob Kerry (D-NE), and Sam Nunn (D-GA)—proposed the USA Tax (short for "unlimited savings allowance"), a de facto consumption tax.[4] It is a tax structure rooted in sound economic theory, good economic evidence, and until recent times, historically bipartisan interest. And, although it is not always the best plan to follow the fiscal policies of the rest of the world, it is certainly worth noting that the United States is the only country in the developed world without some form of consumption tax.

The chief disadvantage of the consumption tax seems to be that it differs significantly from the status quo in the United States. The knee-jerk reaction of liberals is that any tax structure that does not tax income must be "regressive" and therefore clearly unacceptable. Conservatives worry that it would hurt economic growth by raising the price of goods and services. Neither argument has much merit. Try to convince yourself that it is somehow more morally correct or socially progressive to tax the unrealized ability to consume (income) rather than to tax consumption itself, and you will quickly wander off into logical oblivion. We should feel comfortable taxing rich people more than the poor not because they have more Federal Reserve Notes with $20 printed on them, but because of the goods and services they can obtain with those pieces of paper. A stack of $20 bills or a paycheck with a lot of zeroes is intrinsically worthless and only has value to the extent that it can be converted into something you need or want. That is what makes the rich man rich. He can have what he needs and much more of what he wants than the poor man. A consumption tax goes directly after the benefits of wealth rather than its precursors.

While not the focus of this book, I also believe that it is rather easy to make the case that taxing many types of consumption instead of taxing income would yield positive social benefits beyond the increased incentives to save. For example, increased taxes on fuel would cut down on driving and its associated pollution. That is obvious, but there are many other examples of simple daily consumption that have some negative social consequences. For instance, I am within easy walking distance of a Starbucks coffeehouse. I suspect that in about half an hour I will walk there and get a cup of coffee for $2. When I am done with my coffee, I will throw the cup away—another piece of packaging headed for the landfill. But what if the coffee cost me $2.50 instead of $2? Would that change my mind? At an individual level, I'm really not sure, but we can all be sure that if the price of a cup of coffee increased by 25%, demand would fall. These kinds of decisions are repeated by millions of people many times a day. While religious and political views vary widely on the role that consumption should have in our lives, I think the vast majority of people who think carefully and seriously about social problems and opportunities would conclude that some reduction in current consumption, particularly for products related to energy, would be a good thing for the United States overall.

The argument that a consumption tax would hurt the economy is also shortsighted. Indeed, it would create some initial downward pressure on consumption and hence production, but less-fragile consumer spending patterns would likely emerge. Consumption decisions would be more detached from the vagaries of interest rates and other macroeconomic conditions. Higher savings rates would generate households with stronger balance sheets relative to those that are now highly leveraged. In aggregate, we would be trading away some consumption today for our ability to consume in the future. We would be expanding the pool of available capital that is vital for funding new technologies to drive the entire economy forward. It would be a good bargain.

There is no doubt that liberals and conservatives will disagree on the specifics of such a tax. It is, by necessity, neither progressive nor regressive; the details of its implementation govern its political appeal. It can be made more progressive by exempting some agreed-upon items such as foodstuffs or by imposing a greater proportional tax on some predefined luxury items. It can be made less progressive by setting the same percent tax rate for all purchased products and services. Relative to the current tax on income, a consumption tax could be an advantage or a disadvantage to the wealthy.

It is immutable to all the political machinations that would accompany the specific guidelines of a broad-based consumption tax that such a tax would dramatically alter incentives for household savings. Savings would not be taxed. Currently, even the most tax-advantaged savings vehicles either tax savings immediately or defer taxes on savings until some future date. A consumption tax would effectively strip all current and deferred taxes from all types of savings. It would create strong disincentives for the type of consumption behavior that leads to households struggling to manage revolving credit card debt. It has the ability to completely transform the way Americans view savings and debt.

A consumption tax would also encourage more savings among lower-income households. Some of the most popular tax-advantaged investment vehicles such as 401(k)s and Keoghs are tied directly to employment. The benefits of these savings vehicles flow to people with jobs, with less access to those who are unemployed or underemployed.

There are some challenges to be overcome in implementing a consumption tax, which needs to be "fair" and to be viewed as such by the taxpaying public. Because our mental model of taxation has always involved income taxes, in this context, "fair" will likely mean that it is neither more regressive nor more progressive with respect to income than current income taxes. Our basis for thinking about the fairness of taxes may shift over time to mental models that emphasize consumption as the moral basis for evaluating how progressive or regressive a tax is. But for now, our collective psychological anchors are too firmly planted in the current system of income taxes. At a very practical level, a consumption tax needs to be seen as roughly on par with the current income tax system in the amount of money people of different income levels pay to the federal government. It is also abundantly clear that a flat consumption tax of the likes proposed over the last decade in Congress would be regressive relative to the current income tax system unless additional provisions are included that rebate money to lower-income taxpayers.[5] This is because of the simple fact that the wealthy save a higher percentage of their income than the poor and therefore a perfectly flat consumption tax would affect a higher proportion of income among the poor.[6] This challenge could be handled by a combination of product exemptions and rebates. For example, states generally do not tax food and medication, and a federal consumption tax could follow that lead. Tax rebates calculated by multiplying the consumption tax by some percentage of the adjusted gross income for poorer Americans could blunt the impact of underlying disparities in savings rates on the consumption tax burden. If income taxes go away entirely, and therefore no income tax returns are available to determine such rebates, the same effect could be generated by imposing a higher proportional consumption tax (that is, a "luxury tax") on a set of consumption items known to be attractive to wealthier Americans.

It is very difficult to determine the exact magnitude of this tax and these rebates because we have no way of knowing how people would behave under a tax policy that does not exist. However, it is possible to come up with a reasonable formula for rebates, assuming that people in different income tax brackets (in the current system) continue to consume and save the way they do now under a new consumption tax system. However, the whole point of proposing a consumption tax is that it would change the incentives and the patterns of savings and consumption. We presently do not have a solid understanding of how much they would change.[7] However, a sizable group of people who specialize in what is generally called economic structural modeling create models that can make sensible predictions about a proposed policy when there is no historical data of actual human behavior in the new policy regime.[8] This is needed here to determine appropriate rebates.

The same problem—predicting behavior under a tax system that does not currently exist—also makes it more difficult to determine the revenue that would be generated under different levels of consumption tax. We have difficulty predicting revenue under the current system of income taxes—partly due to a near complete inability to project capital gains tax receipts, which are a function of movements in the equity markets—so it should not be entirely surprising that revenue projections under an entirely new tax structure would be complicated. The same structural economic analysis that would yield usable information on the size of rebates would also inform the decision on the exact value of the tax rate.

The bottom line, therefore, is that we do not know enough to determine whether the 15% consumption tax contained in some proposals or the 23% proposed in another is the right number. But it is possible to make educated guesses and to refine our figures with new information.

The second major challenge to implementing a broad-based consumption tax is that it results in the double taxation of individuals who have paid taxes on their income, saved the money for some future date, and now will pay consumption taxes when the money is used for purchases. Imagine that you have paid something like $40,000 in income tax on your retirement savings of $200,000, and then the government turns around and says that the prices of most of the goods and services you need are going up by 20%. You would no doubt be angry that you will end up paying a tax of 40% on that earned money. It is easy to argue that it is a bit unfair to change the tax rules once people who understood those rules have accumulated savings. Of course, any fundamental tax reform would face this problem.

Fortunately, some of the solutions to the transition problem are easy. Money accumulated in tax-deferred accounts, a huge store of wealth for many Americans, would suddenly become money on which no taxes would be owed until it was consumed. There is no real problem handling that money. Posttax savings could be handled by having household savings declared to the IRS and then tax vouchers issued that could be used to pay the consumption tax on subsequent purchases. In all fairness, it is much easier to discuss plans such as issuing tax vouchers than it is to implement them. For example, would you count funds that are stored in home equity as savings and adjust the tax vouchers accordingly? We should avoid glossing over the transition costs; they are real, but the benefit is huge.[9]

We also need to take our tax hats off for a moment and remember some of the psychological and institutional issues that we have spent so much time discussing. Despite the overall low savings rate, one way that many Americans do save effectively is through their employers' tax-deferred retirement savings plans. Reducing taxes on savings to zero by instituting a consumption tax effectively puts savings through an employer-based plan on the same tax footing as saving outside of a plan. Though it may sound silly at first, I think we do need to worry a bit about equalizing the tax advantages completely between employer-based and nonemployer-based savings. Employer-based savings push many of the right psychological buttons that help people to save. That money is automatically taken out of your paycheck before you actually see it and this continues by default until you actively elect otherwise. In our rush to increase the incentives for savings, it would be foolish to completely dismantle the financial and psychological advantages that employer-based savings enjoy. If we determined the correct figures to get the consumption tax completely right and then people decided that savings through the employer no longer looked appealing, we might end up with far less of an increase in household savings.

However, this is not a terribly difficult issue to solve. For most larger companies, there is no issue at all because of the common practice of matching contributions, either dollar for dollar or at some lower level, which creates the immediate incentives necessary to keep the employer as a focal point for savings. At smaller companies where cash matches are less the norm, this is more of a problem. That is why some of the later suggestions about increasing access to retirement savings vehicles for individuals who work at small businesses go hand in hand with my other tax recommendations. Absent these policies, shifting to a consumption tax may have important unintended consequences, which are borne strictly of simple but powerful psychology.

Of all the public policies we consider here, supplanting the current federal income tax system with a broad-based consumption tax is the single most potent policy tool for increasing the savings rate of U.S. households.

Now, for a really cold, hard dose of realism: What if these arguments are for naught and we remain locked in a system primarily of income taxes? Let's assume that the consumption tax proposal never makes it out of Congress. There are still measures we can take within the existing tax structure to facilitate savings.

Create a Low-Cost Retirement Savings System for Small Business Employees

Savings through employer-sponsored retirement plans are a huge store of wealth for American households. The problem is that about one-third of the working population is employed at firms too small to offer a standard 401(k) plan.[10] A given small company may not have an employer-sponsored retirement plan for a variety of reasons, but usually it is too expensive for a private investment management company to administer a program given such a small pool of employees and potential investment dollars. Even if a small company wants to offer such a plan, it is not easy to generate a cost-effective proposal for administration and investment management. In other words, a lot of money can be made by managing the defined-contribution pension plan for Boeing, but what about Crazy Pete's Lawn Care and Snow Removal? We need to find a way that small companies like Crazy Pete's can allow their employees access to some of the same automatic payroll deduction mechanisms that have been so effective at building wealth for employees of large companies.

One proposal that I believe has a great deal of potential is floated by two research fellows—David John of the Heritage Foundation and Mark Iwry of the Brookings Institution.[11] They call their proposed plan the "automatic IRA" (individual retirement account), and it basically entails the federal government contracting with a small group of privately managed mutual funds. These mutual funds, much like those currently offered to federal employees through the Thrift Savings Plan, would agree to accept monies contributed by the employees of small businesses and would hold these dollars in accounts under the names of the individual employees. The investment management company would have to agree to offer a small number of diversified, very-low-fee funds for the plan, and would also have to accept individual minimum balances that are far below industry norms. Contributions would be collected by the employer and then turned over to a government-run central repository that would disperse the funds according to the employee's preferences. If the employee did not make an active allocation decision, the funds would be invested in a prespecified broadly diversified fund. When an individual's balance was sufficient to make him or her an attractive customer to standard IRA providers—carrying a balance of perhaps $15,000—the employee would have the option to roll over this federally sponsored IRA into a private account.

All employers that met some very minimal standards regarding number of employees and length of time in business would be compelled to offer such a program to their employees. The federal government would provide a tax credit to offset the administrative cost of setting up such a payroll deduction mechanism, as well as additional tax credits based on the number of employees who enrolled. The government would also provide employers with the necessary legal forms for enrolling their employees.

John and Iwry also suggest setting a default contribution for employees to an amount other than zero. In other words, unless an employee makes an active choice not to contribute to the IRA, the employer would begin to deduct a statute-mandated contribution amount. While requiring only passive consent will undoubtedly lead some employees to unwittingly contribute money to a retirement plan that they do not even know they have, this seems like a reasonable bit of paternalism to me. The benefit of the opt-in default in terms of increased savings for many small business employees is pretty clear, and the cost would be that a relatively small proportion of them would essentially "save too much" in this account. In other words, a few participants might end up with some savings that they would rather have used for consumption or other investments. But if they truly were unaware that some of their paycheck was being diverted to a savings vehicle, it is unlikely they were considering other investment alternatives that went unfunded because of the automatic IRA. Instead, in all likelihood, setting an opt-in default would cause this small group of individuals, who almost certainly have little financial acumen, to inadvertently delay consumption in favor of increased savings, which does not seem like too high a price to pay.

Allow Poorer Americans to Divert Some Proportion of Their Social Security Contributions to a Government-Managed Stock Mutual Fund

Standard financial theory and basic financial advice recommend that households, regardless of their wealth level, hold some proportion of their funds in publicly traded equities. Holding stocks makes sense for almost everyone, rich or poor, and increases the investor's expected future wealth.

The fact that the incidence of stock ownership in the United States is directly proportionate to wealth should not surprise us. Fewer than 40% of Americans in the lowest quartile of wealth own any public equity at all, and participation among the middle class is modest, at best. The vast majority of Americans in the upper quartile of wealth own either publicly traded stock, interest in a privately held business, or both. Why does the reality of stock ownership look so different from what a financial advisor would recommend? Some of the basic reasons why poorer households do not hold stock are:

- Many of the households that do hold stock own it as part of their employer's defined-contribution retirement plan. In such plans, they may own stocks outright or as part of a stock mutual fund. Americans in the lowest quartile of wealth are less likely to have jobs that provide these kinds of attractive retirement savings options.
- For inexperienced investors, stocks may appear more risky than they actually are. People find risks with unknown probabilities particularly unattractive. Assuming that wealth and financial sophistication are at least somewhat positively related, this means that many poorer Americans may believe that stocks are a big gamble and an inappropriate investment for someone in their financial situation.
- Transaction costs can be high in this market if you have little to invest. In general, those who make small equity investments will pay a significantly higher proportion of their investment in fees and commissions relative to someone investing more.

Poorer Americans would in all probability accumulate more wealth over their lifetimes if they had some exposure to equity markets. The only practical tool the government has at its disposal to generate large increases in stock market participation is the way Social Security taxes are collected and funds disbursed.

I would recommend that all Americans in the lowest 25% of adjusted gross income be offered the option of diverting 3% of their Social Security contributions to a stock mutual fund managed by the federal government. The stock mutual fund, as mandated by federal government statute, would be managed as a pure domestic index fund with no active management decisions other than rebalancing, which is done by the fund custodian. A benchmark such as the Wilshire 5000, a very broad equity index, would be appropriate. Monies would be held in private accounts under the names of individual taxpayers. Disbursements would not begin until the commencement of regular Social Security payments, which would be adjusted downward to reflect the amount of money diverted to the alternate system. At death, the current value of monies held in the account would enter the estate of the deceased.

This is just another way of advocating the politically divisive, partially privatized Social Security system, but with a far narrower scope than the frameworks previously floated. Although we each have our own political predisposition toward this issue, I would like to emphasize the following points:

1. This plan would only be available to poorer Americans. Whether the final cutoff ends up being the recommended 25% or some other number would depend largely on how the program is funded, but I do not recommend that everyone be allowed to participate.
2. The individual who chooses to divert money into a private account would have absolutely no choice in the way it is invested. They could either choose to put 3% of their Social Security tax into the equity index fund or leave it within the traditional Social Security system.
3. The government would have no discretion regarding the companies in which it invested or the weight those companies would be given in the portfolio. The pure indexing investment strategy would be set by statute.
4. Disbursements from these private accounts would be more restricted than those commonly found in private defined-contribution plans; in particular, no borrowing against such funds would be permitted. Also, disbursements could not begin before the commencement of regular Social Security payments.

This is not intended to forward a particular broad political ideology. Rather, it is a narrowly tailored plan designed to solve a specific social problem of considerable importance. In 2001, Sweden, the first nation in the world to implement a universal government-run retirement system, decided to privatize part of its pension program. Facing many of the same problems endemic to the current U.S. Social Security system, Sweden decided that personal accounts were the best way to help workers gain a safe and comfortable retirement. The plan presented here is not nearly as broad as the reforms undertaken by Sweden.

The primary risks associated with implementing this system are (1) it would involve diverting monies from a currently underfunded Social Security trust fund and (2) if participants who contribute to the alternative system end up losing money in the long run, there is the potential for political pressure to bail them out. A number of reasonable proposals exist that could ameliorate the funding problem of the current Social Security trust fund. Prime among these proposals are recommendations to increase the age at which participants become eligible for payments to better reflect the reality of our increasing life spans and to reindex the annual increases in benefits to prices rather than wages. The goal here is not to set out a detailed proposal for solving the funding problem. Many others have examined and written about this problem and the proposals are as varied as the political philosophies from which they emerge. But it is worth noting that fundamentally this is not an intractable problem. If the benefits of equity ownership for poorer Americans could be communicated to the public in a clear and convincing way, it could open the door for some of the other changes necessary to shore up funding for the traditional system. Reindexing and increasing the minimum retirement age become pills that are politically easier to swallow if the benefits to the poor are made vivid to the average voter who may only be, at best, casually interested in Social Security trust fund finance.

Some of the specifics of the proposal set forth here could ameliorate concerns about the possible political pressure to bail out individuals who may have lost money in these equity accounts. This proposal is sufficiently narrowly defined to avoid this pressure in large measure. Political pressure from retirees would be most acute in a situation where the equity markets suffered a major and prolonged decline, not the market's typical year-to-year volatility. Steep and long-lived market declines do not happen in a vacuum; they occur because something fundamentally bad has happened in the U.S. economy or in the world. In such a case, overall tax receipts collected by the federal government would drop precipitously. Even if incomes remained largely intact during the decline, which is an unlikely prospect, the decrease in tax receipts from capital gains would be substantial. Given the current state of Social Security (and Medicare) funding, even those in the traditional Social Security system would likely see a cut in benefits. It is completely unreasonable to believe that a steep and prolonged market decline would not generate cuts in federal funding for entitlements. In other words, in a very bad economy, both equity holders and those holding traditional government Social Security annuities would likely be in the same boat. And in anything other than a very prolonged poor equity market, we can expect those less-fortunate Americans who invested some of their Social Security money in private equity-only accounts to be better off.

There are two other important points that have a bearing on the amount of political pressure that would be generated by a prolonged poor equity market. One is that individuals cannot make investment choices with the account. They can either opt in or opt out, but may not choose among various asset classes. The program is defined this way because the specific problem we are attempting to solve is the lack of equity ownership among poorer Americans. Adding a long-term bond fund would not help achieve that goal. But it is also true that because there are no other investment options, it is not credible to argue that you were somehow confused by the different options available. The program is both simple and abundantly clear; there are no complex portfolio allocation decisions to be made. The other important point is that the amount eligible to be invested in private accounts is the minority of an individual's, and an employer's, overall contribution to Social Security. The majority of the money would still be used for a government-backed annuity.

Require Investment Companies (Mutual Funds) to Disclose the Dollar Amount They Charge on an Individual-Level Basis

When you go to a grocery store to purchase a can of green beans, you are confident that you know exactly how much it will cost. The price is printed on a label, and it is abundantly clear to most shoppers what $1.29 means. Likewise, when shopping for a new flat-screen television, it is easy to understand what $2,999 means. Of course, the salesperson may try to sell you an extended warranty or other add-ons, but those can be declined. If the tag says $2,999, you can be confident that this is what you will pay, plus perhaps some sales tax or, in the future, a wisely adopted consumption tax. Pricing in the market for consumer goods is reasonably transparent and there are federal laws that assure the prices you pay for the goods you receive.

The same certainly cannot be said of the market for financial services. It would be hard to find another service marketed to the general population that has a more confusing price structure. Do you know even the *approximate* dollar amount that you are being charged by any of the companies with which you have mutual fund investments? Do you know the dollar amount you are paying for annuity products? How about the total amount your bank charged you in fees last year? You could probably find the prospectus of one of your mutual funds buried in a file drawer along with your account balances and use that information to get an idea of what these companies charge you, but do you actually ever do that? Chances are that you do not, and neither do most other Americans.

In table 4.1, I have reproduced the fee information for the Fidelity Blue Chip Value Fund. This information was gathered from the fund's prospectus on Fidelity's Web site. The table contains the *exact* information regarding fund fees, in the same format that Fidelity provides to potential investors in the fund.[12]

Suppose you had a $50,000 IRA investment held entirely in the Blue Chip Value Fund, and you invested an additional $100 per month via an automatic payroll deduction. How much would you expect this fund to charge you in fees over the next three years? There is nothing esoteric about this question; it is what millions of Americans should be asking themselves every time they invest in a mutual fund. The problem is that the answer is not so easy to compute: you have to (1) assume that the overall expenses of the fund will remain stable, (2) take an educated guess at your rate of return over the time horizon, (3) multiply the monthly (not the given annual) expense ratio by the expected amount that you will have in the fund that month, (4) add up that sequence of 36 monthly charges, and—if you really want to do it right—(5) discount the fees that you will be charged from the present value of those fees using a "net present value calculation."

Even if you do all of that, the answer you get will only be approximate, because fees are taken out on a daily rather than monthly basis, and no one really knows what your actual rate of return will be. Add to

Table 4.1: Mutual Fund Fee Disclosure

Fee Table

The following table describes the fees and expenses that are incurred when you buy, hold, or sell shares of a fund. The annual fund operating expenses provided below for each fund do not reflect the effect of any reduction of certain expenses during the period.

Blue Chip Value	Management fee	0.54%
	Distribution and/or Service (12b-1) fees	None
	Other expenses	0.43%
	Total annual fund operating expenses[A]	0.97%

[A] Effective February 1, 2005, FMR has voluntarily agreed to reimburse Blue Chip Value to the extent that total operating expenses (excluding interest, taxes, certain securities lending costs, brokerage commissions, and extraordinary expenses), as a percentage of its average net assets, exceed 1.00%. This arrangement may be discontinued by FMR at any time.

This example helps you compare the cost of investing in the funds with the cost of investing in other mutual funds.

Let's say, hypothetically, that each fund's annual return is 5% and that your shareholder fees and each fund's annual operating expenses are exactly as described in the fee table. This example illustrates the effect of fees and expenses, but is not meant to suggest actual or expected fees and expenses or returns, all of which may vary. For every $10,000 you invested, here's how much you would pay in total expenses if you sell all of your shares at the end of each time period indicated:

Blue Chip Value	1 year	$99
	3 years	$309
	5 years	$536
	10 years	$1,190

A portion of the brokerage commissions that a fund pays may be reimbursed and used to reduce that fund's expenses. In addition, through arrangements with Blue Chip Growth's custodian and transfer agent, credits realized as a result of uninvested cash balances are used to reduce custodian and transfer agent expenses. Including these reductions, the total fund operating expenses would have been 0.93% for Blue Chip Value.

Source: This table was taken from Fidelity's online prospectus for the Blue Chip Value Fund. In general, the mutual funds marketed and managed by Fidelity have fees that are lower than industry averages.

this the fact that many investors will have trouble converting an annual expense ratio into a monthly ratio and then adding up their monthly charges. Even making a crude approximation—multiplying the annual expense ratio by the current balance—would elude most investors. That kind of fund fee disclosure does not provide any real transparency into the actual dollar amount that is charged, and therefore just does not work for many investors.

Is Fidelity—one of the true behemoths of the mutual fund industry—just being difficult by disclosing fees in a confusing way? Not really, at least relative to the competition; what you see in table 4.1 is very close to any open-end mutual fund that is marketed to the public. The format and content of the disclosure is mandated by the U.S. Securities and Exchange Commission (SEC). Fidelity is therefore just following the rules and conventions of the industry as a whole.

My own research in this area strongly suggests that the currently required SEC disclosure is inadequate, partially resulting in the fact that investors do not pay enough attention to the fees their financial services providers charge. This negligence costs the American investor a substantial amount of money.[13] Arthur Levitt, chairman of the SEC from 1993 to 2001, used to be fond of quoting the same statistic in his speeches about mutual funds: "On an investment held for 20 years, a 1% annual fee will reduce the ending account balance by 18%."[14] Given the huge popularity of mutual funds as an investment vehicle, that represents a substantial transfer of wealth from private household savings to business profits.[15] And perhaps even more importantly, it dulls price competition in this marketplace.

How do we remedy this? It would be wrong to impose price controls—regulate the fees that mutual funds may charge. We can be reasonably certain that imposing price caps in that marketplace would generate unintended consequences, the most serious of which would likely be a market supply reaction that would limit the availability of those investment vehicles to people with little income or wealth. For example, companies that market and manage mutual funds would find it unprofitable to serve a client who might only be able to invest $500 in a fund if the asset management fees, expressed as a percent of assets under management, were restricted to be the same as those for a client investing $500,000. Much like the competition for high-net-worth individuals among boutique wealth management firms, mutual funds would refocus their business activities toward recruiting and retaining only the top end of the market. That target marketing would not only include traditional tools such as advertising but would also undoubtedly include increasing the minimum investment required to access a given mutual fund. One of the truly great social consequences of the rise of mutual funds has been the accompanying democratization of the stock and bond markets. The proportion of U.S. households that have access to financial markets through mutual funds, and only through mutual funds, has grown tremendously over the past couple of decades. That represents a substantial store of wealth for moderate- and even lower-income households. Decreased access to those funds would undoubtedly have a chilling effect on the savings and wealth prospects of many Americans. Federally imposed price controls would be an unwise bargain.

During the academic year 1999–2000, I left the halls of Carnegie Mellon University to take a position in the Office of Economic Analysis at the SEC. I arrived at that job with the chutzpah and naiveté that often accompany an academic who is working in an area closely aligned with his research. At one of my first meetings with the head of the Investment Management Division, we discussed some potential rule-making possibilities for improving SEC-mandated mutual fund disclosure. Improving disclosure was a priority for then chairman Levitt. "Why don't we just require mutual funds to state, in dollars, how much they charged a given investor last year?" I asked. "They could just put it on the annual statement they give their investors or something like that." I don't remember the exact words the head of the division said at that point, but I know they were calm, seemed carefully chosen, and conveyed that basically that was a really bad idea. Subsequent conversations I had with people within the SEC and with people from the Investment Company Institute (ICI, the main research and lobbying organization for the mutual fund industry) always ended up about the same. The only attempt at a cogent explanation of why this would not work was that the information systems used by mutual fund companies could not track fees at the level of the individual investor or that such tracking would be too expensive.

That was probably a baseless argument then and it is definitely an unfounded argument now. Given the state of today's current marketing information systems, which can compute your expected lifetime financial value to Eddie Bauer as a function of what type of scarf you purchased, it is not credible that mutual fund companies could not rather easily determine the fees and hence the profitability of any investor who holds shares in their funds. The problem here is not faulty or costly information systems, but highly entrenched incentives. If mutual fund companies showed investors the actual dollar amount they charged, the public might not like what it saw. Price transparency and the market's invisible hand would produce heightened price competition between mutual fund companies, where now there is very little. When it comes to fee disclosure, the prevailing attitude among mutual fund companies seems to be: What investors don't know won't hurt them. But, in fact, what investors don't know *does* hurt them.

A good case study of that very effect is the long-distance telephone market. Before Sprint's 10-cents-a-minute plan, callers faced a confusing set of price structures. To determine which company offered the best value, customers were required to have a detailed understanding of their own calling behavior as well as the different options each company offered. Sprint was the first company to simplify its pricing plan to 10 cents a minute, period, regardless of the time of day or number of minutes used. This plan sparked near-epic competition in the industry, with AT&T, MCI, and Sprint each scurrying to offer the best rates to potential customers. The key to the competition was an initial jolt of price transparency from a fierce competitor (Sprint) attempting to erode the market dominance of a historically powerful player (AT&T). Price competition between mutual fund companies would be a boon to individual investors, and over the medium and longer terms would contribute significantly to net household savings and wealth.

I was certainly not the first person to think of price transparency in the mutual fund industry. At about the same time, Representatives John Dingell (D-MI) and Michael Oxley (R-OH) had asked the U.S. General Accounting Office (GAO) to study that very issue and recommend any regulatory changes that would benefit individual investors. The GAO produced a 132-page document that outlined price trends in the industry and argued that price competition would be more robust if price transparency were improved. Specifically, the GAO study made the following recommendation:

> This report recommends that the Chairman of the Securities and Exchange Commission (SEC) require that the quarterly account statements that mutual fund investors receive include information on the specific dollar amount of each investor's share of the operating expenses that were deducted from the value of the shares they own.[16]

The GAO report was sent to the SEC. About 10 months later, the GAO received a reply from the director of the Investment Management Division. The official response included a rejection of the idea to provide individual investors information on the actual dollar value of the fees they paid:

> The GAO recommended that the SEC require mutual funds' quarterly account statements to include the dollar amount of each investor's share of operating expenses. The GAO Report acknowledged, however, that there are advantages and disadvantages to this recommendation and suggested other alternatives for enhancing investor awareness and understanding of mutual fund fees, in view of the additional costs and administrative burdens of such an approach. Recognizing the compliance cost associated with a new personalized expense disclosure requirement would ultimately be borne by the fund shareholders, and may be considerable, we embrace one of your alternative suggestions, namely, disclosure of the dollar amount of fees paid for standardized investment amounts.[17]

The resulting mandated mutual fund fee disclosure—the dollar amount of fees paid for a standardized investment amount—looks exactly like the Blue Chip Value Fund (table 4.1); this is good news for the mutual fund industry, but not for individual investors.

I view this particular public policy proposal as being the most unambiguously beneficial for the American individual saver and investor and, in many respects, the easiest to implement. The SEC has the regulatory power to implement this change without additional legislation; it is completely within their jurisdiction.

Strengthen the Warning Statement about Past Returns in Mutual Fund Disclosures

You are undoubtedly familiar with the standard disclaimer that, by law, accompanies any mutual fund disclosure: "Past performance does not guarantee future return." This is one of those mind-numbingly familiar statements that our brain tends to tune out. It's like those "do not eat" warnings on a bar of soap, a jar of petroleum jelly, or a box of laundry detergent. You figure that some idiot must have actually eaten one of these things at some point, gotten appropriately ill, sued the company, and won.

The downside to this kind of mandated warning and disclosure is that we ignore it. We overconfidently believe that these warnings are written for people who are less intelligent than we are. We tell ourselves that everything will be fine if we just use a little common sense. After all, when something looks like a bomb and we purchased it precisely because it explodes, we don't really need to be told, "Light fuse and get away; do not hold in hand."

In contrast to many of these ridiculous warnings, however, the warnings about mutual fund investing need to be ramped up significantly. When we read the mandated warning "Past performance does not guarantee future returns," most of us either don't process that information or dismiss it as something the lawyers probably were required to write. After all, our pattern-seeking minds tell us that if a mutual fund manager was good at picking stocks for the last few years, there must be an above-average chance that he or she will continue to be good at picking stocks for the next few years.

Within a given asset class of mutual funds (stocks, bonds, and so forth) past performance is the single largest determinant of where an individual investor will decide to invest his or her savings. By comparison, investors typically ignore important information on taxes and fees.[18] The problem is that according to the best available evidence—which is unusually strong and has been replicated with many different sets of data—past performance of a mutual fund has no material predictive power for future returns. Mutual fund managers cannot consistently outperform passively managed indexed funds, in which they simply pick stocks to replicate a given stock market index rather than make trades based on beliefs about the likely performance of a given stock.[19]

Evidence is not confined to the academic literature that long-run superior performance of actively managed mutual funds is lacking relative to passively managed index funds. John Bogle, founder and former CEO of Vanguard Inc., the second largest complex of mutual funds in the world, has become something of an evangelist for the idea that low-cost investing through index funds is the best investment strategy.[20] He built Vanguard Inc. around this idea, so he is not an entirely impartial observer, yet the institutional studies he details in his book, along with the sizable number of academic studies on the issue, collectively provide compelling evidence that past performance simply does not matter.

Why, then, has this idea not found its way into SEC-mandated disclosure and the general beliefs of the saving and investing public? There are both psychological issues and business tactics at play that are designed to enhance some common psychological mistakes. Basically, people search for and believe that there is causality in apparent patterns, even when there is absolutely incontrovertible evidence to the contrary. We just cannot help this evolutionary propensity, which is reinforced regularly by advertising messages that tout the past performance of mutual funds. The investment companies advertise past performance because it works,[21] and money flows rapidly into mutual funds that have advertised their recent good performance.[22] Of course, the mutual funds that are advertised are not randomly chosen. A large complex of funds will tend to advertise those that have had good recent past performance and not the ones that have done relatively poorly. In some cases, in a practice known as "incubation," they may start several funds with different investment strategies but eliminate those that have done poorly prior to their public availability. By exploiting the random chance that some funds will actually beat their passive benchmarks over any given time period, these marketing practices conspire to make the messages we see about past performance appear to support the idea that some funds, and some fund complexes, are able to consistently generate superior performance. And because we are innately inclined to believe this message, it works exceedingly well.

The SEC should change the mandated disclosure on mutual fund prospectuses to include language such as "Past performance does not predict future returns." Certainly I do not believe that individual investors would wake up one morning, start reading their new prospectuses, notice that the word "guarantee" has been dropped from the old disclosure, and suddenly become more attentive to the fees and taxes that should be important in their decision-making processes. But changing disclosure in this way would undoubtedly spawn articles in the popular press, conversations on money-oriented talk shows, and other public messages calling attention to the fact that the SEC does not believe past performance really matters. Far more than directly reading the prospectus, the media has the potential to steer some savers toward examining their mutual funds in ways that would be constructive. The power of the media may be turned to the advantage of good decision making rather than working against it.

However, there are entrenched interests here that can be expected to resist such a recommendation. Investment companies cannot charge the same level of fees for a passively managed index fund as they can for an actively managed fund that has been advertising its recent superior performance. Fees mean jobs and wealth for the company and, of course, the company has a powerful interest in protecting its wealth—which is ironic, since they are ostensibly concerned with the investors' wealth. The ICI would lobby both the SEC and relevant committees of Congress in an attempt to keep such a change from occurring; there is too much money on the line to expect anything else. The ICI would present research in an attempt to cast just enough doubt on the broad consensus of the relevant academic literature that the SEC would hesitate to change the law.

Reinvigorate the Marketing of U.S. Savings Bonds

Mutual fund disclosure is an important issue because such a broad cross section of the American public invests in mutual funds of one type or another. There are, however, many households that do not invest in mutual funds, stocks, bonds, or any other asset that provides the potential for reasonable long-run returns. The most valuable asset of these

households may be the promise of future Social Security benefits and perhaps a little equity in their homes.

A few years ago, I had a consulting job with a large retail bank. During
one of my trips to the bank, the vice president of marketing (VP) explained the features of the bank's new customer service system for its call
center. One of the new features was that once a caller keyed in an account
number, the system was able to determine how profitable a customer he
or she was. It was a fairly sophisticated system, using information on different account balances as well as cost estimates from various transactions
that the customer had previously made with the bank. If the system determined that you were a very profitable customer, your phone call would be
moved up in the queue. If, on the other hand, the system determined you
were a relatively unprofitable customer, your call would be placed at the
end of the queue and your place in that line could be jumped by more-
profitable customers. The bank was not concerned that less-profitable customers would probably become annoyed at the inordinately long wait and
might take their business elsewhere. The system operated as a stealth
method for eliminating bad customers and retaining good ones.

When the VP explained the "customer service" system to me, my immediate reaction was that it seemed to violate the basic fairness principle
that, profitability aside, people should be served in order. First come, first
served is a well-entrenched cultural norm. The VP, noticing my failure to
embrace the new system as a stroke of business genius, went on to insist
that such a system was absolutely necessary. "The standard 80/20 rule isn't
true in retail banking," he said.[23] "You make 120% of your profits on 80%
of your customers and then you lose money on those last 20%."

It is difficult to condemn the bank for its behavior. In many ways, it was
doing what other consumer product–oriented companies do—they work
hard to create products for those willing to pay them a lot of money, and
market less-attractive options to those who are unwilling or unable to do
so. For example, Procter & Gamble will sell you Tide laundry detergent if
you are willing and able to pay for that premium product; if you are not,
they will sell you Gain. The difference between a savings account and
laundry detergent is that it is hard to argue the broad social consequences
associated with buying Gain. We don't lie awake at night worrying about
the poor neighborhood kids who had their jeans washed in Gain rather

than Tide. But basic access to capital markets takes on a completely different social dimension. We should worry that there is a sizable group of people whom banks and other financial institutions find it unprofitable to serve. Such a group almost literally cannot save.

Peter Tufano and Daniel Schneider, both on the faculty of Harvard Business School, provide substantial evidence that that is the case.[24] Banks and other financial institutions are interested in having you as a customer if the revenue you generate exceeds the marketing costs of acquiring and retaining you. For example, let's say that $50 is the total cost associated with tracking your transactions, answering your telephone calls, mailing you statements, and printing and sending you marketing information. Assume also that the financial service provider makes 2% on the money you give to them; this money could be coming from the spread between the interest rate you are receiving and the interest rate at which they are lending money, as in a bank, or the annual management fee you are paying on a mutual fund.[25] In this case, the company would need you to deposit at least $2,500 ($50 ÷ 0.02) just to break even. There are many U.S. households that do not have $2,500 in savings; in fact, there are many households that do not have $1,000 in savings. If people do not have the money to present themselves as profitable customers, they are faced with additional fees or minimum investment requirements they cannot meet.

Those additional fees and barriers to investment for individuals of more meager means is a fundamental difference between price discrimination in the market for financial products and services and price discrimination in other markets. In many other markets, charging different prices to different groups of people is socially beneficial. That is, we make some products and services available according to an individual's ability to pay. For instance, student and senior citizen discounts at movie theaters are socially beneficial forms of price discrimination for a service—seeing a movie. Because students and senior citizens often have lower incomes, the value of a dollar to them is higher than the value of a dollar to a middle-aged, employed person. So, instead of charging everyone $6 to see a movie, theaters charge $8 for people who are not students or senior citizens and $5 for those who are. They do this because they make more money by extracting a larger profit from those who can afford it and charging a bit less, while still earning a profit, from those who cannot. In so doing, however, they effectively transfer some wealth from a group that has more to one that has less. This is a well-known principle in economics—price discrimination generally operates in such a way that the profitable strategy for a business also has a socially beneficial outcome.

However, this generally well-founded principle breaks down rather dramatically in the market for financial services. If you cannot meet a minimum requirement for a checking account, you are charged more than if you can. If you have less money to invest in a mutual fund, you have access to a restricted set of funds, which normally have higher annual management fees than those available to people who have more money. That is socially beneficial price discrimination turned on its head; the poor man pays more than the rich man.

I recently moved my primary checking account from a regional bank to a local credit union. My monthly paycheck is now deposited directly into my credit union account. Nevertheless, I did not immediately close my account at the regional bank. There were some monthly bills being withdrawn automatically from that account, so it was important that they were discontinued before the account was finally closed. In the two intervening months, my average balance in that account ranged from about $600 to $800. In each of those two months, the bank charged me a $16 account maintenance fee that I had never paid before. It is useful to contemplate those numbers for just a moment and reflect on their implications. Because I am a reasonably well-paid professional and my directly deposited paycheck met some minimum dollar requirement, the bank did not charge me for purchasing what is arguably their most basic account.[26] They even paid me a paltry amount of interest. If my economic circumstances were different such that $600 to $800 was the amount I regularly could keep in my checking account, the bank would annually charge me $192 ($16×12 months) in account maintenance fees. Assuming my average account balance was $700, that represents a simple interest rate on my money of $-\$192 \div \$700 = -27\%$! So, I would be paying 27% of my capital just to hold the account. That is a horrible burden for poorer Americans to bear and creates stark disincentives to saving. Public policy cannot reverse that reality entirely, but it can take steps to ameliorate the problem.

Reinvigorating the marketing of U.S. savings bonds would offer some practical help for this problem. In a world of increasingly complex financial products and services, savings bonds are almost an anachronism. Tufano and Schneider have referred to savings bonds as a "quaint oddity," which I believe is an accurate description of the way most people view them.[27] Originally marketed to help finance war efforts, U.S. savings bonds became the savings tool of the low- and middle-income masses. They were very safe, easy to obtain, and helped demonstrate the saver's patriotism. Perhaps most importantly, they were available in small denominations, and following World War I, the U.S. Treasury continued their promotion in order to "make war-taught thrift and the practice of saving through lending to the Government a permanent and happy habit of the American people."[28] And that began the effort to consistently market U.S. savings bonds.

These simple, low-cost savings instruments are available through many employers, although it is doubtful that their employees actually know about it. Savings bonds generate little excitement in the investment community because they generally have long maturities and relatively low interest rates. There are no real incentives for employers to market them; their presence as an investment option remains obscure relative to the heavily marketed options of many defined-contribution pension plans. The U.S. Treasury has scaled back its marketing support for U.S. savings bonds and has closed some offices that helped promote them.

Given the high cost of accessing savings vehicles for many lower- and lower-middle-income families, it would behoove the federal government to take measures aimed at actively promoting savings bonds. Because these instruments are often distributed through employers, there is ample opportunity for public-private partnerships to help accomplish that goal. A relatively straightforward solution would be to provide business tax incentives to offset any money a company needs to spend for marketing and distributing savings bonds to its employees. Even relatively small amounts of money spent trying to raise the awareness of savings bonds would go a long way to generate interest.

Create a Matching Savings Plan for Low-Income Individuals

In our current income tax structure, one of the central problems with tax incentives for savings is that they are aimed at wealthier people.

Those who pay little or no taxes—those with the lowest incomes—see no benefit from the kinds of tax-deferred savings vehicles we have been discussing. To those in the 30%+ marginal tax brackets, the benefit of the ability to save pretax dollars is obvious. Proposals to raise the limits on 401(k) or IRA contributions may expand the aggregate pool of savings in the United States, but provide little in the way of answers about how to increase the savings rate among Americans of more modest means.

The Saver's Credit program, a federal program adopted in 2001, is an attempt to enhance savings incentives for lower-income households. Its main feature is a rebate of up to 50% on federal taxes for dollars contributed to IRAs and 401(k) plans. For example, if you contributed $1 to an IRA and you were eligible for a 50% rebate, then in addition to the normal tax benefits of the IRA, you would receive a 50-cent rebate on your federal taxes. It was conceived and acts as a type of federal matching plan for savings.[29]

Matching plans have a great deal of intuitive appeal; in addition to being financially attractive, they tend to push the right psychological buttons that spur us to save more. They are very simple to understand and the benefit is obvious. It cannot get much easier than "For every dollar I put in, the government puts in 50 cents." Some of the psychological benefits are also immediate. When I do decide to save, I see my account balance increase by more than the amount I invested. It appears to be instant free money. Compare that with a standard tax-deferred instrument such as an IRA: the benefits of receiving compound interest on the deferred tax monies is substantial, but the gains accumulate over time, and moreover, it is hard to determine the exact dollar value of the benefit at any given point of time. In other words, it's complicated. It is nothing like "For every dollar I put in, they put in 50 cents."

The Saver's Credit program has that nice matching feature to it, but suffers from a number of serious problems that limit its usefulness as a policy tool. The most serious of these problems is that it is very complicated to figure out how much match money you are eligible for. Complex programs have little hope of achieving their aims, particularly with lower-income households that may already have a serious problem with financial literacy. Also, the income eligibility thresholds are quite low, shutting out many of the households that could benefit most from a well-structured matching plan.

One recent experiment on a new type of matching program appears to hold promise for providing a more effective alternative to the Saver's Credit program.[30] A group of researchers set up an experiment at 60 H&R Block offices in lower- and middle-income neighborhoods in metropolitan St. Louis.[31] Each of the 14,000 individuals who filed taxes through these offices was offered an opportunity to contribute money to an IRA, either using out-of-pocket money or funding it with their tax refund. Some filers were also offered a 20% cash match for any contributions to the IRA, while others were offered an even more generous 50% match. The availability and magnitude of the cash match made a difference. Of those who were not offered the cash match, only 3% contributed to the IRA. Those who were offered the 20% or 50% match contributed at rates of 8% and 14%, respectively. Tax filers in the control group (no match) who did contribute to the IRA invested an average of $765, while those who were offered a match of either size (and took the offer) contributed an average of about $1,100. Unsurprisingly, those filers who were expecting a larger refund were more likely to contribute. In a theme that emerges repeatedly, it is much easier to save money that you have never held in your hand. The psychological difference between money that belongs to you but that you have not yet taken possession of and money you actually possess is enormously important in predicting savings behavior.

This experiment demonstrates in a convincing way that in low- and middle-income environments, a clear and easy-to-understand matching-funds program can increase savings rates and contribution levels. But that tells only part of the story. It is discouraging that even though the absolute level of participation under the matching programs was substantially larger than the 3% participation rate in the control group, only 14% of filers contributed to an IRA when offered a 50% cash match. There is no magic bullet here. This kind of matching program helps, but it appears not to motivate a large group of people to do what is almost certainly in their best interest.

Linking a potential match to an income tax return is not the only way we might begin to think about a practical government-funded matching plan. A few years ago, I was involved with a charitable organization that wanted to help poorer families in the Charlottesville area save enough money to be able to make a down payment on a home. The organization received grant money from the State of Virginia that allowed them to set up accounts into which the participants could save money while receiving a 300% cash match from the program. In this particularly generous version of a savings-matching program, participants had to agree to use the money within a prespecified period of time to purchase and occupy a home. They also had to agree to attend a series of financial education seminars that covered a wide range of household financial management topics. The charitable organization was responsible for receiving and depositing participant contributions and monitoring attendance at the required seminars.

My impression was that this type of targeted matching program administered by a private charitable organization worked reasonably well. Its goal, to get low-income families into owner-occupied housing, would likely lead to additional wealth accumulations for these families—their mortgage payments would act as monthly forced-savings vehicles and the values of their homes would appreciate over time. The plan's structure was very simple for the participants to understand and the benefits were obvious. The required financial education, while a bit paternalistic, made practical sense given the participants' lack of basic financial literacy. The charitable organization responsible for administering the program, staffed almost entirely by volunteers, approached the task with great enthusiasm. In short, this seems like a particularly effective way to spend tax dollars to help poorer Americans save more money.

Emphasize Skills Important to Savings in High School Curricula

When I was a 15-year-old student at LaSalle High School in Cincinnati, the Christian Brothers who ran the prep school decided that all students should take a half semester of typing. I thought to myself: Typing! I am in the Advanced Placement track, for God's sake! I am a smart kid who is supposed to do interesting things with my life. Surely, if typing is necessary, I will have someone else do that for me. My obvious destiny is to continue my studies in Latin, English, and mathematics—not learn how to do clerical work!

I was being literally sophomoric, of course; it did indeed turn out to be very useful. And while it is no great cause for celebration, I am reasonably sure that I'm still one of the fastest typists among my colleagues. I'd love to know how many hours I have saved over my lifetime because of that requirement. The school administrators were cognizant of the increasing role that computers were beginning to play and decided that their students would not hunt-and-peck on keyboards all their lives.

The language of financial literacy in the United States is Microsoft Excel. While there were early competitors, most notably Lotus, Excel has emerged as the clear winner in the struggle to become the standard product for basic and advanced financial analysis. Excel is a software package that allows easy manipulation of sets of numerical data. It also has automatic, built-in functions that make financial analysis much simpler than if you had to complete the tasks by hand. At Darden, all students are required to demonstrate competency in Excel prior to beginning the formal MBA program because this skill is considered so fundamental for even the most basic financial analysis. Most people do not go to business school or become financial analysts, but the need for basic financial acumen has never been more important for the economic well-being of middle-income Americans. The average U.S. household today makes many more financial decisions that are more complex than at any point in history. We need to come to the collective realization that the tools of basic financial literacy should be an integral part of a sound liberal education.

Computer software and applications make theoretical formulas and constructs more accessible and meaningful to today's average teenager. It does not take appeals to academic studies to come to the inescapable conclusion that technology is interwoven into the lives and decision making of younger Americans in more potent ways than ever before. There is little doubt that this will continue to increase over time.

Consequently, we need to connect a socially important subject area with the tools and pedagogy that will motivate and internalize the learning of our students. In my view, basic instruction in Excel is currently the most sensible way to do that. If a different software package or technology becomes the dominant tool of basic financial decision making, we should allow our pedagogy to shift toward those new ideas and technologies.

Using Excel to introduce basic education in financial analysis into the high school curriculum is largely a matter of local control. While the federal government does mandate some school programs, curriculum control is largely left to local school boards. To be practical, this idea would have to be implemented by convincing local school boards that learning this material is in the best long-run interest of current high school students.

Bernheim, Garrett, and Maki (1997) studied the effect of state-level education mandates that started in the 1960s. During that period, some states required that specific elements of financial education be included in the high school curriculum. The topics included practical skills such as household budgeting, money management, savings and investing, and the use of credit. Savings and investment education covered the relationship between risk and return, and the roles of inflation, taxation, and diversification in portfolio choice. In 1995–1997, the authors sought to determine whether this education had any discernable effect on the adult financial behavior of these students. In short, their analysis of these 2,000 adults provided evidence that financial education does persuade people to save more.[32]

Because of the differences in people's general planning ability and the impact this planning has on savings, it is also clear that instruction in basic concepts of household finance, particularly when paired with the use of common financial software, enhances an individual's ability to make sensible household budgets, compute how much money he or she will need to retire, and perform a number of other organizational and computational tasks that research suggests will help grease the wheels of long-term financial planning and savings.

Beyond exposing students to software programs that allow data analysis and basic household finance, they should also be taught the basic mathematical tools that will help them later in life to make reasonable financial decisions. Prime among these tools is the ability to calculate compound interest. I am certain that one of the reasons many Americans save so little is because they fundamentally do not understand how interest compounding works and hence underestimate the value of savings. Understanding compound interest is inextricably linked to making reasonable estimates about how much you should save for retirement, determining how much it is really costing you to borrow money, and a host of other questions that are important in good financial decision making.

Basic interest compounding could be taught in an early high school algebra class. Something as simple as the following question would help students understand the basic idea that it takes less time to double your money than one might think: If you save $100 today in an account that has a constant annual interest rate of 10%, how long will it take to double your money?[33] There are also ample opportunities to introduce more advanced versions of this concept in other mathematics classes such as calculus. While the simple algebra-based examples can provide very good approximations of what would actually happen in financial markets, calculus-based versions are more accurate in certain situations. The point here is to emphasize that interest compounding provides the opportunity for an entirely different set of useful examples that are perfectly compatible with the underlying mathematics being taught. It also provides some variety to the textbook examples, which are often very heavy in physics and engineering applications.

Closely linked to the mathematics of compounding is the concept of the "present value of money," the analytical technique that allows us to determine the real cost or benefit of payments either *from* us or *to* us that occurs over a period of time. It allows us to answer questions involving financial transactions that will occur over time, such as: "Would it be worth paying some money up front to refinance my mortgage?" and "How much money will I need to retire?" Again, examples of present-value-of-money calculations could fit neatly into a number of different mathematics classes that are already staples of the high school curriculum.

While both of these techniques are offered as built-in functions of software packages such as Excel, understanding the analytics behind them would allow younger Americans to develop a refined intuitive understanding of the benefits of savings and the dangers of debt. Even though most of them would probably forget the equations, the remaining ideas would be powerfully and beneficially instructive in some important life decisions.

The Low-Hanging Fruit

Some things are easier to accomplish than others. Major tax reform and Social Security reform are hard. Adding a federally sponsored retirement plan for small businesses is not as difficult, but developing and implementing the management and oversight structure for the private mutual funds that would comprise the plan's investment options is not child's play. That fruit is hanging about halfway up the tree. The real low-hanging fruit is changing mutual fund disclosure laws, particularly with respect to fees, and beefing up the marketing of U.S. savings bonds. The former can be implemented directly by a government regulatory agency with an act of Congress; the latter would require some funding, but is not fundamentally complicated.

We should move immediately to implement mutual fund disclosure law and savings bond marketing. We must look for political opportunities for fundamental tax reform, Social Security reform, government-sponsored matching programs for low-income savers, and changes in government-mandated high school curricula. Government action can undoubtedly help to increase household savings, and these are good places to start.

5

A CEO'S GUIDE TO INCREASING
EMPLOYEE SAVINGS

Well-formed public policy is a potent tool for increasing savings. But the front line in the battle to increase household savings is the workplace, where people make many of the decisions that will affect their savings and long-term economic prospects. Private enterprise can also make substantial inroads here. A small business owner or senior executive in a large corporation can take some simple steps to increase the savings of his or her employees. If those steps become known as best practices, the effects could ripple throughout the U.S. economy.

In this chapter, I follow three overriding principles in dispensing some practical advice for business executives who have some paternalistic instincts toward their employees. First, because you are businesspeople with broad responsibility within your organizations, I'll assume you already know that advice such as "Increase your contribution to your employees' 401(k) plan" is not particularly helpful, and what's more, those kinds of proposals are expensive. If you want to spend more money on your employees' benefit packages, you don't need me to urge you to do that. Second, it would be equally useless to advise that you require your employees to save a certain percentage of their income. Some of your employees would likely view such a plan as an infringement on their personal freedom, and this would put you at a competitive disadvantage in the marketplace.[1] I prescribe ideas that preserve an employee's personal financial freedom, even if that means allowing individual choices that we might view as foolish. Third, I am assuming that people are unlikely to get much smarter in a short period of time. Despite the good work of many organizations that offer free financial advice and education, people will probably retain their same biases and make the same mistakes. The prescriptions detailed here do not assume any dramatic shifts in people's cognitive ability when faced with complex financial decisions and, in fact, the efficacy of some of the advice relies squarely on the persistence of those predispositions. I try to make those biases work in favor of rather than against the individual.

If you do not have any paternalistic instinct toward your employees, you should nevertheless find this chapter beneficial. Broadening participation in and increasing employee contributions to employer-sponsored pension plans can directly benefit the company itself. It is clear that the old defined-benefit pension plans common at many companies for most of the twentieth century increased employees' tendency to remain with a given company and hence effectively reduced employee turnover. There is increasing evidence that defined-contribution pension plans have the same effect, although there is no obvious economic reason that this should be the case.[2] Employees vested in a defined-contribution plan can always roll their pension money over into a private tax-deferred vehicle (e.g., an individual retirement account), suffer no financial loss, and seek employment elsewhere. But the interesting psychological effect of accumulating money within an employer-sponsored pension plan appears to extend well beyond that. In economic-speak, the effect appears to stem from the fact that workers' discount rates and productivity rates are negatively correlated. This is just a very academic way of saying something you have probably known for a long time. Some of your employees have a strong work ethic, which extends beyond their desire for a weekly paycheck. They work hard because that is who they are; it is part of their worldview and defines for them what it means to be a good person. These are the same people who tend to take the long view of things, to put off immediate gratification in order to slowly build a better life for themselves some years down the road. You want to keep these people on your payroll. They are very productive. They also happen to be motivated by well-funded, well-designed pension plans because they place a great deal of value on the future payoff of those plans.

You also have other workers who want everything and want it immediately. They tend to be your less-productive workers and if they left, it

would not be bad for your business. Because they want everything immediately, and have high discount rates, they tend to be unmotivated by generous pension plans.[3] These less-productive workers are also more likely
to leave the company to access the lump-sum distribution option offered
by defined-contribution plans. Therefore, in addition to making your
workers financially better off, a good pension plan has the effect of sepa-
rating the proverbial wheat from the chaff, of retaining your better employees and implicitly coaxing your less-productive employees to leave.

So let's begin with a discussion of defined-contribution pension plans,
and how you can make yours better.

Choose a Pension Plan Provider with Low Fees

The federal law governing private-sector retirement plans, the
Employee Retirement Income Security Act (ERISA), requires that
those responsible for managing retirement plans (called fiduciaries)
carry out their responsibilities prudently and solely in the interest of the
plan's participants and beneficiaries.[4] The fees assessed by the provider
of your 401(k) plan are subtracted from the value of your employees'
savings and are an important issue over which to exercise careful fiduciary oversight.

Mutual fund fees vary widely. Annual management fees for widely held
equity funds commonly range between 0.2% and 2.0%. The fees for funds
that concentrate their holdings in high-grade bonds vary somewhat less,
but the differences among the fees charged by companies can be significant. There is no evidence that funds with high management fees provide
a better net return to investors than funds with lower fees; in fact, there
is a good deal of evidence that the opposite is true.[5] Low fees are likely to
be a reliable indication of higher net investment returns over the long run
and they affect the value of your employee's retirement account in eco-
nomically significant ways.

To clarify this, I have constructed a very simple example (figure 5.1).
Consider two employees, both of whom invest $10,000 per year in a stock
mutual fund within their employer's 401(k) plan and achieve a 10% per
year gross rate of return. One employee invests in a stock fund that
charges no front-end load and a 0.2% annual management fee, while the

other invests in a fund with a 3% front-end load and a 1.2% annual management fee. I have graphed both employees' wealth accumulation over a 20-year investment horizon.

How different are their ending cash balances? The ending value for the employee in the high-fee fund is $520,341, and it is $613,269 for the employee invested in the low-fee fund. That is a difference of about $97,000, or 18.6% more wealth for the employee in the low-fee fund. It is the kind of money you could use to retire the mortgage on your house.

Mutual funds held within an employee-sponsored retirement plan may have all of the same fees associated with standard retail mutual funds: front-end loads, back-end loads, annual management fees, 12(b)-1 fees, and so on.[6] In addition, investment management firms may charge a plan administration fee that would either be billed directly to the company, to individuals within the plan as a flat annual fee, or deducted from the net return of employee shares, much in the same way the annual management fee is deducted. The point here is that these fee structures can get confusing and without careful attention, both your company and your employees can lose significant amounts of money before

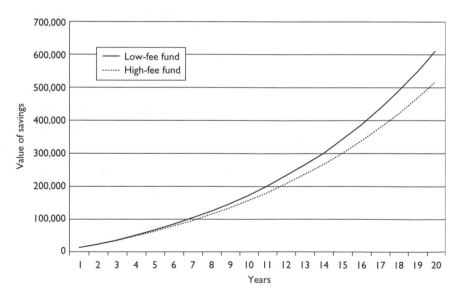

Figure 5.1: High-fee versus low-fee mutual funds
Source: Author.

they even realize that they are in a bad financial situation relative to other marketplace offerings.

The U.S. Department of Labor offers a very useful template called a Uniform Fee Disclosure.[7] This is a handy instrument for evaluating the fees assessed by alternative retirement plan providers and keeping fiduciaries from getting lost in the shuffle of complex and opaque fee structures. Although this kind of comparison work is detailed and tedious, there is no doubt that your employees' retirement wealth can be considerably enhanced by carefully scrutinizing fees charged by current and potential retirement plan providers.

Limit the Number of Mutual Funds Contained in the Pension Plan

Pension plans that contain a large number of investment choices work to the detriment of investors. Too many choices are more likely to confuse individual investors and delay both their participation and asset-allocation decisions.[8] When people become overwhelmed by too many funds and too much data, their natural tendency is to decide not to choose.

If you do not believe that your employees may find the options in your defined-contribution pension plan confusing, ask your human resources manager for the information new employees receive, or attend their benefits orientation. If the prospectuses of the various mutual funds and annuity options are not included in the packet handed to you, ask for them. Assuming you can get them quickly, stack them up on your desk and then go through them. If you find yourself puzzling about the exact investment strategy of a given fund or the particular structure of an annuity that is being offered, just imagine what some of your employees are going through. You hired them because they each had a particular expertise. They may be very smart, but they are not likely to have a clue about the difference between Sallie Mae and U.S. Treasury bonds. The more options you throw at them, the more difficult this already daunting task becomes. You can simplify it for them.

A properly diversified portfolio does not require many choices. Basic needs can be covered by access to mutual funds specializing in (1) cash or cash equivalents, (2) fixed-income securities, and (3) domestic equities. It can be argued that it makes sense to include mutual funds that hold (4) foreign securities, (5) real estate, (6) small capitalization stocks, and (7) life-cycle funds that automatically adjust the asset mix of the portfolio as the employee moves closer to retirement. Some participants will also want access to an annuity product, but that list just about spans the reasonable alternatives. Pension plans with many choices invariably have funds whose asset holdings overlap each other. The same underlying portfolio could be synthesized with far fewer funds and without the confusion that accompanies such a large set of choices.

Choose to offer the fewest number of investment options that span the necessary asset classes for a properly diversified portfolio. If there is more than one financial service provider offering products that are included in your deferred-tax retirement plan, these companies will undoubtedly pressure you to offer more of their products to your employees. So that they will not miss out on the investment money that an employee might place with another provider, they will want to saturate the plan with all the possible products that any employee might find attractive. Remember, it is not in your employees' best interest to have a large number of inevitably overlapping products to choose from. Exercise your instincts to limit their options and they will ultimately be better off.

Two good examples of companies that accomplish these goals are TIAA-CREF (Teachers Insurance and Annuity Association–College Retirement Equities Fund), the pension provider for universities, hospitals, and nonprofits, and the Thrift Savings Plan, which is available to federal employees. They have few choices, but those choices are sufficient for a well-diversified portfolio, and their fees are very low. These two plans serve their investors well and are good models for private defined-contribution pensions.

Do Not Take Payments from Financial Service Providers in Exchange for Offering Their Products in Your Tax-Deferred Retirement Plan

Accepting payments in exchange for access to your employee's investment dollars is, in my view, a breach of the fiduciary responsibility required by the U.S. Department of Labor for companies that sponsor these types of plans. Nevertheless, I believe that this occurs with disturbing frequency. A plain reading of the law requires companies to act solely in their employees' best interest when designing a retirement plan. It is hard to construct a scenario under which accepting payments in exchange for the privilege of marketing financial products to employees enrolled in the plan would constitute a reasonable exercise of fiduciary responsibility. The monies transferred to the company could otherwise be used to reduce fees for products contained in the plan, which would certainly be in the best interest of employees.

Set the Default Asset Allocation in Your Tax-Deferred Retirement Plan to Something Other than 100% Cash

For many pension plans, if the employee does not elect an asset allocation, the "no choice" option or default is to place 100% of company contributions into a money market account. For the vast majority of employees, this asset allocation makes no sense.

Many companies use this as the default allocation largely for reasons of legal conservatism. Setting the default to all cash can be defended as the "safest" investment choice for employees, virtually guaranteeing that their principal will never decline in value. But this is only the safest portfolio allocation under the narrowest possible definition of safety—capital preservation. The real rate of return on that concentrated portfolio is likely to be below the rate of inflation, which leads to negative real returns for the investor. Employees who have all of their retirement savings in cash will indeed preserve their capital, but their spending power will not be preserved.

Also, many employees will leave their pension money in the default allocation of the plan.[9] Perhaps they are busy and don't want to take the time to change the asset allocation, even if the transaction costs associated with making such a change are generally low. It is also reasonable to assume that some employees believe the company is making decisions in their best interest. Since companies do have fiduciary responsibility with regard to employee pensions, this is not a completely unreasonable assumption, but it is often wishful thinking. It is also clear that a substantial proportion of employees do not understand what an allocation of 100% to a money market fund really means. Recall our conversation about financial literacy in Chapter 3 and the John Hancock study that found that two out of three defined-contribution pension fund participants did not know that money market funds do not contain stocks. Is it any wonder that many people do not reallocate their pension monies away from 100% cash?

Companies are not specifically required to use 100% cash as the default option in their pension plans. In the years since the Enron scandal, the Securities and Exchange Commission has focused its regulatory attention on companies that aggressively market their own stock as an asset alternative for their employees' retirement plans. The abuses of this kind of behavior are well known, but beyond the requirement that employers act in the best interest of their employees, they are largely free to set up retirement plan defaults however they see fit.

A default allocation divided into thirds between equities, bonds, and cash would better serve employees. This allocation would fall in line with common financial advice for many more employees than current pure cash defaults. It bears repeating that setting the default would in no way restrict the employee from choosing a different fund mix and asset allocation; it would simply occur if the employee decided not to choose. Barring a sudden and widespread uptick in financial acumen, we can rest assured that many people will not make a choice.

Another alternative to the equal division between stocks, bonds, and cash is the use of life-cycle funds. These funds, which are marketed by a number of mutual fund complexes, automatically adjust the portfolio mix of the fund as the investor ages. Funds for individuals who are a long way from retirement typically are invested heavily in equities, while those whose investors are closer to retirement hold a greater proportion of fixed-income assets. In that sense, a fund is specific to a particular age group. A mutual fund complex that includes life-cycle-type funds will generally have several, each with a different target retirement date for the participant. Therefore, for a 30-year-old employee, a life-cycle fund with a targeted retirement date of 2040 would be about right. Employers could set the default allocation of their pension plans to 100% in the life-cycle fund whose targeted retirement date most closely matched an employee's 65th birthday. That would generate asset allocations, and projected retirement savings, that are in most cases far better than the current practice allows.

Set Defaults on 401(k) Plans So that Employees Are Automatically Enrolled Unless They Explicitly Choose Otherwise

More troubling than the default allocation, however, is the reality that many employees will not enroll in the company 401(k) plan.[10] My advice here is very simple: set up your human resource systems so that new employees are automatically enrolled in the 401(k) unless they specify otherwise. By law, companies that set an automatic enrollment feature for their defined-contribution retirement plans must defer at least 3% of an employee's salary.[11] The maximum is 10%. The minimum employee contribution steps up 1% each year for three years so that a 6% minimum must be deferred in the fourth year. Also, employers must provide a contribution matching plan that contributes at least 3% to employee savings in addition to the deferrals of the employees themselves, and these contributions must vest in no more than two years. Consequently, automatic enrollment is not an option for companies that do not contribute to their employees' retirement plans, but it is an option for companies that currently either provide matching funds of at least 3% or contribute at least 3%, independent of employee contributions.

A couple of points should be emphasized here. First, setting the default to include a contribution on the part of the employee is a highly paternalistic approach with potential risks. Financially naïve employees—or those who do not pay much attention to what is going on with their paychecks— would be unwittingly contributing money out of their regular pay to a pension plan that they had never considered or consciously joined. A few may be in financial situations where contributing to such a plan makes little sense, but because the default is set to include a contribution on their behalf, and they are not paying close attention, they may end up somewhat financially worse off. For example, an employee trying to save money for a near-term business venture may want to keep as much of his or her savings out of age-restricted funds as possible. While this type of situation could certainly arise, I deeply suspect that only a very small minority of employees would be negatively impacted. Even those who were inattentive would not become financially worse off in tragic ways; the money would not disappear, and they would still get the match. On balance, it is clear that the benefit to employees who would otherwise not enroll or receive the matching funds far outweighs the risks to a comparatively small group of people.

Second, this approach will almost certainly cost your company more money. The objective is to increase participation in a program that has direct costs for every participant. If your company can afford it, that's great; but if the additional costs are unreasonable given your company's financial situation, you might consider scaling back the amount you match for new employees so that the cost of the new program with more aggressive defaults matches your old program. In essence, by scaling back the contribution but encouraging more participation, you are transferring some wealth from those who are more financially savvy, and would have maxed out their contributions under the old system, to those who have less financial know-how. Everything being equal, this seems like a pretty reasonable trade-off. After all, we are trying to boost the savings of employees who are most vulnerable to shortfalls later in life. This would be effective in that respect and at the same time not decrease the aggregate monies being transferred from your company to the employees' retirement plan.

Targeted Financial Education

Education is often held out as the panacea of many social problems. People would wear seat belts if they knew it would save their lives; they would be more careful with matches if they realized that carelessness causes forest fires; and they would stop smoking if they really understood that cigarettes cause cancer. Since we know that people do not always do what is in their best interest, education is not the end-all solution—but it certainly helps.

There are several nonprofit organizations that have made it their business to help people understand the benefits of saving more money. Most notable are the American Savings Education Council, the Employee

Benefit Research Institute, and Choose to Save. These organizations have provided the public with valuable information and tools via online retirement savings calculators, advertising, and pamphlets that describe savings alternatives.

Many companies do spend resources educating their employees about money and savings—at a minimum, they inform their workers about the options in their pension plans. It seems reasonable to ask two questions about this kind of education. First and most basically, does it work? Do people make better financial decisions once they have been exposed to employer-sponsored financial education? Second, what can be done at the level of the individual company to make the resources spent on education more effective?

To answer the first question, some types of education do appear to help employees make better financial decisions, whereas others do not. In particular, printed material and information distributed in employee newsletters are largely ineffective, while employee workshops and seminars are successful.[12] If you think about that result for a moment, I suspect it will not come as a complete surprise. What could be more boring than reading some financial planning advice in an employee newsletter—advice that many of your employees will (correctly) believe has been picked over by your legal staff? On the other hand, having someone talk to you about your financial plans and potentially answer your questions is not nearly as tedious. In the world of financial advice, one person talking to another matters.

Employers can also leverage the socially pervasive behavior of talking about money to increase the effectiveness of their employees' savings plans. Although referencing exact dollar figures is considered impolite and often veiled, people love to talk about money. Much of what many of us know about savings and investment comes from conversations with others. Coworkers are especially important because the financial situations faced by people who work together are more likely to be similar. Information that is effectively communicated to one employee is therefore likely to find its way to others.[13]

Who, then, should be targeted for employee-based financial education? The facile answer is everyone, but two groups may especially benefit. First, look at women with below-median incomes. Men are often overconfident and stubborn, to their detriment, when it comes to financial issues,[14] whereas women are more accepting of advice that is given in financial education seminars.[15] Also, because women tend to outlive men, their golden years are particularly at risk for financial shortfalls.

Second, employers should select a group of employees, men or women, who are opinion leaders within the organization. These employees are not only smart; other people in the company typically look to them for advice. An opinion leader is viewed as being competent along some important dimension and is approachable. In some ways, these employees can be viewed as natural leaders; others just naturally pay attention to them. Marketing types have understood this concept for a long time and, indeed, it is the basis for a marketing tactic that is called "viral marketing" in reference to the spread of disease. The concept itself is simple—a person infected with a dreaded communicable disease who never leaves home is not much of a danger to the public, but if that person were a frequent flyer, he or she would become quite a threat. Similarly, in marketing, if Nike can get its new basketball shoes onto the feet of people who are considered in the know for the latest street-wear fashions, the product will diffuse out into the broader marketplace more quickly. It is the same basic idea for sales of basketball shoes, the spread of infectious disease, or the transmittal of valuable financial knowledge—it spreads much faster if those who initially have it are in contact with a lot of other people.

How will you find the opinion leaders? Talk to a few people, and I'm convinced you can identify them. If those in your organization cannot identify its emerging leaders, you have larger issues to deal with than who should attend financial education seminars.

Finally, there is the issue of what should be communicated. The complete pedagogy of a financial education program cannot be included here. But, I do want to point out a few basic topics that deserve special consideration and one financial product that needs more educational attention. Beyond the logistics of enrolling in an employer's pension plan, the most basic notion that employees should take from a seminar is how much money they need to retire. This amount should not be a number that pops out of some online calculator, but one that comes from another person who sits down with the employees and walks them through their assumptions and thinking about retirement. Advice from another person is more likely to be trusted and acted upon. But I also think there is a danger inherent in this type of analysis and communication. The very large dollar figure that emerges may appear absolutely unattainable. And when people see a goal that appears beyond their reach, some will not even try; they give up before they begin. That is why it is important that this retirement discussion and analysis also include information that will halt this slide toward financial apathy and surrender. Employees must understand, very clearly, the power that compound interest has to help them achieve their goals.

There is no doubt that many people do not understand how compound interest operates, and it is probably not possible to teach the mechanics of how it works in a reasonable time frame to employees who have never considered financial issues. However, it is not necessary that they understand every last detail of compound interest to grasp the basic principle that saved money can grow at a much faster rate than they might currently imagine. Figure 5.2 is a very simple graph that can help you illustrate the point without diving into any complex mathematical details. Whether you use this graph directly or create your own, keep in mind that the simplicity of the graph matters; do not make it complicated. The figure depicts the savings growth over a 30-year time horizon of two individuals, each earning $50,000 per year, one who has chosen to save 3% (light gray area) of his or her income and one who has chosen to save 6% (dark gray area). The graph assumes 8% annual growth in assets. The 6% saver ends up with about $400,000 and the 3% saver with $200,000. You may not find these numbers shocking, but they may surprise an employee who is considering a savings plan.

You could get much more complicated here, for example, by correcting all dollar figures for projected inflation. But I think it would be most powerful to show your employees that the dollar amount they will need for retirement is large, while simultaneously showing them a very simple graph that vividly displays how large their savings can grow. This analysis can be easily customized for the individual with graphs produced for a given income and savings level. Keep it simple and, to the extent possible, keep it graphic.

One class of products that generally receives insufficient attention in basic financial education is annuities, while at the same time they are

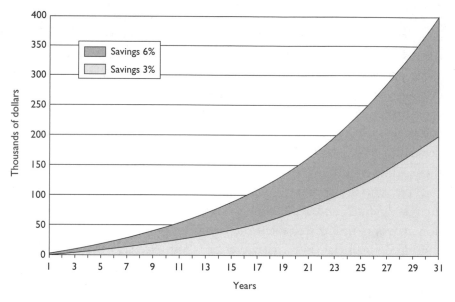

Figure 5.2: Returns to savings
Source: Author.

provided as an option in many retirement plans. Annuities come in many shapes and sizes, but the basic product is designed to guarantee the recipient a known, fixed income for life in exchange for an initial up-front investment. They are becoming more popular because many people prefer the absolute certainty in monthly income that annuities provide relative to the vagaries of determining the appropriate monthly draw from a self-managed portfolio.[16] I have criticized mutual funds for the complicated fee structures they throw at potential savers. Annuities' fee structures are also obscure, essentially buried in the difference between the expected income stream generated by investing $X in a very low-risk asset, and the amount that would be received by purchasing an annuity. The difference is the profit to the business that is marketing the product, which is often an insurance company. It is difficult for any individual to determine the expected cost of investing in an annuity. One thing is certain—if you live long enough, annuities are good investments and if your life span falls short of actuarial averages, it is a bad deal for you.

Added to that ambiguity is the large variety of products available. You can purchase a single-life policy, which pays a fixed amount per month until the day you die; a double-life policy that pays until both you and someone you designate (that is, your spouse) die; or you can choose to have the payment cut in half once one of you dies. Also available are products that have surety periods so that if you and your spouse get hit by a bus immediately after paying a huge amount of money to purchase an annuity, some amount goes to your heirs instead of it being completely lost to the annuity provider. The list goes on, and it is difficult to know what to do.

James Poterba, an economist who has done a great deal of research on individuals' retirement decisions, has examined the market for annuities with an eye toward determining how expensive they really are.[17] He finds that if you live about the average length of time, they are not a very good deal. But an interesting issue surfaces when he looks at the cost not to the average person in the population, but to the average person who purchases annuities. It seems that people who purchase annuities tend to live longer than those who do not. One of the reasons for this is because these individuals have private information about their health. This is what economists call the problem of "adverse selection." In other words, if I know something about my health, I can also make inferences about the probability that I will live a longer or shorter life than average, and that information informs my decision as to whether an annuity makes sense for me. Insurance companies worry about that. Standard actuarial tables can mislead them about what to expect in their annuity pool.

Because people really enjoy having stable monthly incomes, and many annuity products are purchased near the time of retirement, we can expect a marked climb in the demand for these products. It is important that employers talk to their workers about the different annuity options available. It is also essential that those who talk to employees about annuity products have a frank discussion about the employees' health, even though this can be a very personal and sensitive subject. Such a discussion would not require an individual to divulge details about his or her health, but it would raise and link the issues of health and annuity products in ways that would likely enhance the clarity of the employee's decision making.

Give Detailed, Personalized Financial Advice

When I was hired by the University of Virginia, like many people starting a new job I attended a benefits orientation session. It covered a lot of ground, but among the issues on the agenda was an explanation of the employer-based retirement plan, in this case, a defined-contribution 403(b) plan.[18] During the session, several people asked questions about the investment products offered in the plan. For the most part, these questions centered on mutual fund and annuity products offered by TIAA-CREF and Fidelity Inc. (the large mutual fund provider). Many questions focused on the differences among the various funds offered, what mix of funds made sense for a given individual, and whether it was wise to contribute additional money to the plan (beyond what the university would automatically contribute).

The facilitator, while certainly both prepared and wanting to be helpful, was obviously afraid to say anything that might even come close to helpful financial advice. When a new assistant professor in the Sociology Department asked whether it made sense to contribute some of her income to the tax-deferred savings plan, the facilitator reluctantly said something like, "Well it depends on your own individual financial situation." Of course, this is obviously true, but it also completely ignores the reality that for the vast majority of people in a position similar to this 30-something new assistant professor, the answer should be an unequivocal "Yes!" Unless she had large stores of wealth somewhere, of which she would be completely aware, putting some pretax money in this plan would make a lot of sense. At this point, one arrogant participant, a new faculty member at Darden, just could not take it any longer. He raised his hand and proceeded to answer her question in the affirmative. Everyone instantly began asking him questions and, perhaps foolishly, he began to answer them—very directly.

Answering people's questions on the spot was not nearly as daunting as it might sound. They were not asking about the subtleties of the average maturity or yield on a given bond fund. They wanted to know things like whether the retirement plan was good or bad. Should they make additional contributions to it? Should they just keep everything in a money market fund (the default allocation of the plan) or should they fill out one of the forms being offered to change the allocation? The facilitator could have offered some very concrete and sound advice in responding to these questions, such as: The retirement plan is indeed a good one. Yes, in most instances saving some additional money through the plan makes sense. No, an allocation of 100% to a money market account is probably not smart except in some special financial circumstances. The problem was not that we had an ignorant facilitator, but that the facilitator was afraid of being sued.

At that point in 2001, federal regulations issued by ERISA disallowed employers from giving financial advice to their pension fund participants. These regulations were well-intentioned; there was a concern that employers would provide advice to employees that was in the best interest of the company and not the employees. For example, a company could advise employees to hold a large proportion of their retirement portfolio in company stock or to allocate money to mutual funds provided by an investment company that was paying what amounts to a kickback to the employer based on the amount of money employees invested in their funds. These were certainly reasonable concerns, but at the same time, disallowing any financial advice about retirement plan decisions to pass from employer to employee cut many people off from one of the best places they might receive good financial information.

The Pension Protection Act of 2006 changed the landscape of federal regulation in this area, but it remains to be seen if businesses will implement many of the changes that this law allows. Particularly pertinent to this discussion, under the Pension Protection Act, ERISA-covered retirement plans can offer participants financial counseling through a registered investment company, registered broker or dealer, bank, or insurance company acting as a fiduciary. In short, this means that the companies you contract with to provide financial products and services to your plan are now allowed to give financial advice to individual employees.

To protect participants from the aforementioned conflicts of interest, any payments that occur between you (the employer) and the financial services provider must be independent of the product choices your employees make. Also, advice about a particular portfolio allocation must be based on a third-party certified computer model. The employee provides information about his or her particular financial situation to the financial service provider, who must use that data and the computer model as the basis for recommendations. Advisors must also disclose compensation, potential conflicts, past performance of plan investment options, available services, how participant information will be used, and the fact that participants can get advice from an advisor not affiliated with the plan.

This new law is a very reasonable compromise between conflict-of-interest concerns and the realization that it is natural to receive financial advice about retirement plan choices from one's employer. It also allows one person to sit down and talk to another when seeking advice—and this tends to work.

Implement Forward Contracts for Savings

In many respects, the crux of the savings problem in the United States revolves not around confusion with regard to the pricing structures of financial services or misplaced tax incentives, but rather the simple fact that people have trouble giving up immediate consumption. Saving is hard because it requires sacrifice, and sacrifice is a tough sell—even to yourself.

But what if we didn't have to sacrifice today in order to make the decision to save more? Perhaps we could dampen the pain of going without by committing ourselves to save more—tomorrow. Tomorrow we will have more money, so it should not be as difficult. That is the logic behind an ingenious set of recommendations by Bernartzi and Thaler in their "Save More Tomorrow" plan.[19] In a nutshell, this plan offers employees the option of committing to a future increase in their contribution to their employer-sponsored retirement plan. The key is that the increase will take place at the time of their next scheduled raise in salary. So instead of taking an immediate pay cut to fund additional savings, employees are essentially committing to a smaller increase in their take-home pay so they can increase their savings. They are buffering the pain of sacrifice by pairing it with a larger increase in their ability to purchase. Bernartzi and Thaler implemented this plan at several companies, including a midsize manufacturing concern. In what is perhaps the most startling set of statistics of the entire implementation analysis, the preprogram pension contribution rate of those who took part in the program was 3.5%. Eighty percent of those who started the plan continued with it for at least four years. The average contribution rate of those who stayed with the plan rose to 13.6%. It is too early to tell if those results can be replicated in a large number of companies, but it is an understatement to say that the results are promising. The psychological effect of allowing people to precommit to saving more in the future — when their income increases — appears to be powerful.[20]

Extending this logic to other situations is straightforward. While we often concern ourselves with the plight of those who have less money, we all know people who have perfectly reasonable incomes but cannot manage money or keep themselves out of debt. Sometime each year, everyone who earns more than about $90,000 gets what looks like a raise; this occurs when they hit their Social Security (FICA) tax ceiling. Suddenly, their monthly or biweekly paycheck increases. Just like the raises of workers in manufacturing firms, the FICA tax limit could be used as the "gain" necessary to mask the pain of future sacrifice. I am not aware that this has ever been tried in any setting, but if it worked for raises, it would likely work in this situation as well. This is an amazingly simple thing that you could do with your own employees, requiring little more than the paperwork you already have on hand for employee retirement plan participation and allocation decisions.

Limit Your Own Conspicuous Consumption

I saved this one for last, because I suspect some of you will cringe upon reading the title of this section. For all our talk about not violating the personal financial freedom of your employees, I'm now going to come dangerously close to infringing upon yours.

Your consumption matters in the savings rates of your employees. Like it or not, you are in their reference group and some of them aspire to be like you. Your employees notice the kind of clothes you wear to work, the car you park in the lot, and the description of your last vacation. They know where you live. They know if you belong to the most expensive country club in town. You may not think they pay attention, but they do.

And when they see conspicuous consumption or relative frugality, they infer that you view others with similar consumption patterns more favorably. This is a difficult concept to measure and to my knowledge no one has done it with any degree of certainty, but we know from our experience as people that we tend to view those who have our same opinions and tastes as smarter than those who do not.[21] It is hard for us to believe that a person who agrees with most of our ideas and choices is an idiot. Likewise, it is easy to believe that someone who comes to different conclusions than we do about life's choices is just a little less thoughtful and less intelligent. There are good reasons for employees to agree with their bosses, and not just on ideas expressed in the workplace but in taste and consumption decisions as well. You like people who are like you.

Furthermore, consumption decisions can form what some economists have termed an "information cascade" within the organization.[22] If you are a CEO, a line worker may not know much about you. But those who immediately report to you know what club you belong to, what kind of house you live in, and what kind of car you drive, and they make consumption decisions based partly on their desire to seem more like you. That, in turn, can cause a ripple effect through the entire organization, as each person looks to his or her boss for consumption cues. It is well-known that some companies have developed cultures of conspicuous consumption, whereas others are much more frugal. At which type of company do you think it is easier to save if you are a secretary earning $30,000 a year?

6

A HOUSEHOLD GUIDE TO SAVING

This is *not* a chapter about investment strategies. If you would like to know about investment strategies, there are limitless books on the subject that range from the thoughtful to the ridiculous. Instead, in this final chapter, we ignore the public policy makers and CEOs and talk about your personal saving habits—what the psychologists and economists say you are likely doing wrong and right. I won't tell you that you should save more money or use credit cards wisely. I assume that if you have gotten this far, you are already thinking seriously about these issues and don't need me to extol the virtues of saving more or avoiding consumer debt. Let's discuss some practical advice for you and even for me, so that if the public policy makers and CEOs ignore my recommendations, at least we will have a better understanding of what we do right and what we likely do wrong when we think about our own savings.

While I do not talk about investment strategies designed to make you rich, I do identify investment and financial behavior that will likely cause you to lose money, or draw down your savings. If you have saved it, you presumably want to keep it, and what we have discussed with regard to common psychological mistakes in financial decision making does have a lot to say about what we should avoid in the market for financial products and services.

Make Sure that Mental Accounting Is Working for You and Not against You

While mental accounting may violate some basic economic rationality, we all do it. When we think about how to spend or save our money, the context of the transaction makes a difference. We need to make sure that the tricks our brains play on us work to make us richer instead of poorer. Here are a few everyday ways to accomplish this.

When you decide to save, make sure that your idea of what constitutes savings makes sense in a given situation. For most of us, to save means taking an amount of money and placing it in one or more accounts that we have mentally designated as our "savings account(s)." We do not believe we have saved until we transfer money to that set of accounts. For example, my paycheck is automatically deposited into a joint checking account that my wife and I share. We then periodically transfer some money out of it into an investment account held by another financial services provider; that account is highly liquid and includes check-writing privileges. I do not consider money "saved" until it is transferred from one account to the other, which really doesn't make sense. This is an artifact of my own mental accounting, whereby only money placed in certain designated accounts satisfies my psychological desire to save.

This kind of narrow mental definition of savings can cause some very financially counterproductive behavior. In particular, many people regularly contribute to a mentally designated savings account that pays a relatively low interest rate, while simultaneously paying a higher interest rate on outstanding debt. Although they consider paying down their outstanding debt a good thing to do, it does not fill their psychological need to make regular contributions to savings. Holding savings in a low-interest account that is sufficient to pay off a higher-interest debt is what a finance professional might term "negative arbitrage"—giving away money for free.[1] There also seems to be a sense among many people that if they pay down a debt (such as a credit card bill or even a mortgage), the money is "gone" or no longer accessible. On the other hand, savings account funds are considered readily available should an emergency arise. Of course, this kind of thinking makes absolutely no sense. If you have paid down a credit card bill, you could always borrow against it again; and if you had to do this, at least you would have a very clear understanding of why you were borrowing the money, while otherwise the cause might simply be a psychological barrier. Another option for emergency funds is home equity loans, which are exceedingly easy to obtain and have low transaction costs. Paying down high-interest debt generally makes very good financial sense, even if it means a period of zero contribution to what you might think of as savings.

When you decide that making regular additions to savings from your income makes sense, arrange to have that money automatically withdrawn from your paycheck or other payments you systematically receive. Do not receive your entire paycheck—either a paper check or an electronic deposit in your bank account—and then require a separate transaction in which you physically write out a check or make an electronic transfer from your bank account to your savings or investment account. For even the most disciplined among us, creating that separate transaction heightens the psychological pain associated with saving money. Let mental accounting do some work for you; it can trick you into believing that you never really owned that money, that you never really held it in your hand or saw a bank statement that included it. Do not allow yourself the slightest opportunity to get attached to it. Remember, when it comes to money, it is better never to have loved than to have loved and lost.

Leveraging the same psychological phenomenon, when you receive a raise at work (or when you are informed of the timing and magnitude of a coming raise), immediately decide how much of that additional money you would like to save and adjust your automatic deductions, both pretax and posttax savings, accordingly. In the best case, you should have these deductions adjusted to coincide with the first paycheck in which your raise appears. If you can work it out properly, at no time will you receive a regular paycheck that is less than the amount of the previous period. Your new savings deductions will lessen the increase of your next paycheck, but you will never see an actual decrease in the dollars you bring home. You will never see the additional monies that you intend to save, nor will you have time to get used to the extra things in life that this incremental money could buy. And you will fool yourself into saving more.

Mental accounting not only affects the decision of whether or not to save but can also affect asset-allocation decisions in nonproductive ways.

Here is a simple mistake that trips up many people. When we consider asset-allocation decisions, many of us tend to think of investing in stocks with our "long-term" money and in bonds or cash with our "short-term" money. This actually is not a ridiculous mental accounting rule, as it can make a great deal of sense in many situations. However, as we age, many of us hold substantial amounts of money in tax-deferred accounts such as 401(k)s and individual retirement accounts, as well as investments in standard taxable accounts. What can easily happen is that we psychologically assign our tax-deferred investments to the "long-term" account and our taxable investments to the "short-term" account. After all, unless we borrow against our tax-deferred monies, we cannot have access to them until at least 59½ years of age. It is natural to think of those as longer-term investments. The otherwise reasonable mental rule then comes into play: stocks for long-term money and bonds for short-term money. Many of us hold significant stock positions in our retirement accounts and then use our regular non-tax-deferred accounts to hold bonds. This ends up costing people a lot of money because the advantages of tax deferral are much more potent for bonds, which pay out regular dividends, than for stocks, which generate wealth mostly through capital gains that go unrealized until the time of their sale.[2] Stocks held in taxable accounts also have the added advantage of being able to generate capital losses—selling a stock that has lost value—to offset taxes on ordinary income. To the extent that you hold investments both in and out of tax-deferred accounts for a reasonably long period of time, it generally makes sense to hold most of your stock positions in taxable accounts and taxable bond positions in tax-deferred accounts. The economic advantages of handling this savings decision correctly, or at least approximately correctly, are quite significant.

You Really Are Not as Smart as You Think You Are

And even if you really are that smart, it may not help you much when it comes to saving money. You probably believe that your income will keep increasing over time and that you will make investments that produce above-average market returns. I am never going to convince some of you that you ought to assume you are about average when it comes to your career path or predicting the stock market. So let me just point out a few things that ought to set off some warning bells if you notice them as part of your own behavior. If you have these symptoms, not only are you over-confident, but your overconfidence is costing you money.

First, if you are reading financial publications, looking at stock charts, and actively trading stocks, then you have a problem. The more you trade stocks, the less the average return on your portfolio is likely to be.[3] In addition to being assessed brokerage fees, you will pay the bid-ask spread and taxes. It adds up, and in the case of very active stock traders, it can add up significantly. There is a whole industry available to provide information designed to make you a "smarter" stock trader. If you buy and read that information every day for the next 10 years, you will not be better at choosing stocks than someone who has instead spent his or her time doing needlepoint. In fact, there is a good chance that you will make *less* money than your needlepointing counterparts who don't know which stock is headed up or down and who trades only to rebalance their portfolios or for tax reasons. Actively trading stocks is hazardous to your savings.

If you find yourself continuing to sit on a stock that has lost value over the course of several years, this is also a sign that overconfidence has gotten the best of you. When you bought the stock, you thought it was going to increase in value and now the market has proven you wrong. The problem is that you are both confident in your own ability and hesitant to internalize some data that your confidence might be misplaced. Right now, the loss is only on paper, but once you sell it, you have to book it as a loss in your mental accounting ledger. You will have to admit to yourself that you were wrong and, in so doing, you chip away at your own image and it is painful. As long as you don't sell the stock, you tell yourself that its value still might go up, and you won't have to face the incongruence between your beliefs and reality.[4]

The problem with this psychology is that selling a stock that has lost value can often make good financial sense. The federal tax code allows capital losses from stocks that have decreased in value and which have been sold to offset capital gains from other stocks that were sold at a profit or for ordinary income. So, while you are not setting out to generate capital losses when you invest in individual stocks, you should know that given a sufficient portfolio of stocks, some losses are likely to occur.

These losses have financial benefits because of their tax implications, but you will never receive these benefits, or they will be delayed, if you hold onto the losers.

Stocks are just one example of people's stubborn refusal to sell something that they thought was going to increase in value for less than what they paid for it, even if it makes imminent financial sense to do so. The housing market provides another important example. In an upward-trending market, houses may trade hands rapidly, many sitting on the market for only a few days before they are purchased. During periods of a housing market downturn, however, prices often do not correct to clear the market right away. In other words, people ask a certain amount for their house, and when they do not get it, they choose to wait rather than accepting a lower offer. The housing inventory builds up, and the average number of days that a property stays on the market increases, sometimes dramatically. All the while, the owners are either unable to move or they are paying two mortgages, one for the house they moved into and one for the house they have not yet sold (a situation that can be financially devastating). At some point, the market cracks and people begin lowering prices. But for those who are trying to sell a home that they have recently purchased, their mental accounting tells them that just to "break even," they have to get the original price they paid for the house, plus their 5–6% brokerage commissions and some money to cover the transfer taxes and the transaction cost of the mortgage. That's a lot to expect in a down market. And so they hold out for more money, and their savings is rapidly drawn down, particularly if they are carrying two mortgages whose payments are going mostly toward interest rather than principal.

Finally, the other psychological trick that wreaks havoc on some people's savings is the nearly irresistible urge to check the value of their assets frequently. People tend to find the pain of losing a certain amount of money more potent than the joy they derive from receiving the same amount. One practical implication of this is that checking the value of their portfolios frequently tends to make people overly anxious. The values of stocks and bonds increase and decrease, and even if they do tend to go up over time, the pain associated with seeing a daily loss is real. When people become overly anxious about their portfolios, they are more likely to trade assets, and this active trading generally leads to decreases rather than increases in wealth. You will experience more peace of mind if you forego the morning ritual of checking your financial Web sites, and you are likely to be richer for it.

Too Much of Your Savings May Be Getting Eaten Up by Fees and Taxes

Scrutinizing the fees that are charged by the financial products you own and the taxes they generate is a very good use of your time. I begin by returning to my favorite example—the implications of mutual fund fees. Mutual fund taxes are also an important matter to explore because some funds that seem very similar to others may have very different tax implications.

If you are currently holding mutual funds in a regular, rather than tax-deferred, investment account, you will be liable for taxes generated from any dividends the fund might pay or any capital gains generated by the fund as a function of their activity in buying and selling assets. By law, the net capital gains that are generated from the sale of assets within the fund are passed through directly to fund shareholders. In other words, if your mutual fund holds stock in Wilcox International Cement Co. and then sells that stock at a profit, the mutual fund must distribute those capital gains to you and you have to pay taxes on it regardless of whether the share price of the mutual fund itself has gone up or down.[5] This is important to understand because some mutual funds generate a lot of capital gains taxes whereas others do not. Commonly, funds that specialize in assets that produce investment value through their price appreciation (like stocks) produce more capital gains taxes than mutual funds holding assets that pay regular dividends (like bonds). Even within a given class of funds such as stocks, however, the taxable distribution of funds can vary widely. Funds that "churn" their portfolio—actively buying and selling stocks as part of their investment strategy—are much more likely to generate capital gains distributions than funds that take a more passive investment approach, such as index funds. So, actively managed funds often cost you more in terms of taxes, in addition to the higher fees they generally charge as compared to their passively managed counterparts.

The Securities and Exchange Commission has adopted some rules that provide a bit more transparency about the taxable distributions a given mutual fund generates. It now requires the prospectus of mutual funds to display something called "after-tax returns"; by comparing the returns of a given fund with the after-tax return, you can determine how effectively they will avoid generating additional tax burdens for you. But these standardized tables, much like the mandated fee disclosures, make some assumptions that may not fit your particular situation. They are not a perfect gauge of the real cost to you.

The best bet in a situation like this is to stick with passively managed funds when possible, both for fee and for tax reasons. In some situations, actively managed mutual funds that help you minimize the amount of money exposed to the Alternative Minimum Tax (AMT) may make sense. You probably already know whether or not the AMT is something you need to worry about. If passively managed funds are not an option, you should ask about the "churn rate" of the fund, a measure that indicates how often the assets of the fund turn over or how often and in what quantities the fund buys and sells shares in its underlying assets. When comparing two funds, a higher churn rate often means more taxes for you.

Taxes and fees are not exciting, but persistent attention to these two details of the financial world creates big money over the long term. We want your savings to grow, and keeping an eye on these boring details will ultimately prove much more valuable than all the time you might spend trying to figure out what the next hot stock is going to be.

Raise Your Anchor

There is a good chance that your savings rate is being affected by some arbitrary psychological anchors that you never really consider. It would be best to figure out these anchors sooner rather than later so that you can adjust your behavior accordingly. Let me give you some brief advice on where you might begin to look.

The amount your employer contributes to your tax-deferred savings plan—that is, your 401(k)—is almost certainly not related in any meaningful way to the amount of money you will need to save for retirement. The contribution rate is more likely based on what the company can afford and what it thinks it needs to contribute in order to be competitive in the marketplace. All too often, people infer meaning from these contribution rates and use them to help simplify the more complex problem of figuring out how much they will need to save for retirement. There are many retirement calculators available, but the amount you will actually need should be thought of as completely independent from your employer's contributions.

The consumption behavior of your friends and family—your reference group—may have little to do with what is appropriate for you. Remember that your own perception of their consumption is likely to be biased by your imperfect memory, and that consumption information is often exaggerated when it is conveyed. I know that this is hard to do, but it is important. Also realize that in a culture where revealing household financial information is considered taboo, you probably have little idea of exactly what your peers' financial situations really are, how much they are saving, and how much they are in debt. The fact that a friend has a new car doesn't mean that he or she can really afford it. And if that person is average in this respect, he or she is saving less than you should be saving. So what you see and remember about consumption is not exactly reality, and reality itself is not a good model of what would constitute financially responsible behavior.

What you can afford has little to do with what a mortgage broker will lend you for your house (based on your income and savings), what a credit card company will lend you, or whether a bank will qualify you for a new car loan. Determining whether or not you can really afford it requires thinking through your current savings, your current and expected future income, and a series of potentially complex contingencies that may occur in your life. This can be hard, so people look for simple clues or anchors from which they can base their decisions. Just because you take out a mortgage for 20% less than the maximum amount that the bank or mortgage broker is willing to loan you does not mean you are being financially prudent—20% less than lunacy is still lunacy. Financial service providers are not looking out for your savings.

Teach Your Children Well

Frugal parents raise frugal children and spendthrift parents likewise tend to raise spendthrift children.[6] Regardless of family income and educational level, saving money can become an intergenerational habit. Beyond setting a good example ourselves, what are some of the important points that we should teach our children about money? We can now draw on our deeper understanding of the psychology of money to help us come up with some sensible answers.

First, it is abundantly clear that people who are capable of deferring gratification end up better off than those who cannot. This is true not only in the world of personal finance but also in other areas that all too commonly cause problems for teenagers—think sex and drugs. Some of this ability is innate, but we can be reasonably sure that some of it is environmental as well.[7]

The idea of giving a child a fixed allowance from which baseball cards, video games, and ice cream may be purchased seems almost passé in today's world. But until a person is old enough to earn some working income on their own, the only other practical option is for us to make consumption decisions for them on a case-by-case basis: "May I buy the baseball cards?" Yes or no. "May I go with my friends to the movies?" Yes or no. While as a parent you may have some notion of a budget for the purchases and activities of the child, that budget is far enough removed from the child that he or she will not see the trade-offs. However, children will learn financial responsibility more quickly if they have to make those trade-offs themselves by deciding how to spend an allowance. Even a very small amount of money issued as a fixed allowance with a narrowly defined set of potential purchases begins the process whereby the child understands the concept of trade-offs and the benefits of deferred gratification: "If I don't buy the ice cream now, I'll be able to get two extra packs of baseball cards this weekend."

Intimately related to this is the need to demonstrate the added benefits of deferred gratification—in this case, interest. At the earliest practical moment, you should help your child open a savings account into which his or her allowance can be deposited. If the sums of money are insufficient to qualify for an account, you can put the minimum amount in the account yourself and then add your child's money to it. It is important that the child physically go to the bank to make deposits and withdrawals to see the interest that accumulates. We know from psychology that these transactions, and the memories that they form, make a difference. Don't just lump their money in with yours and tell them that it's there. Have them become mentally and physically engaged in the process as much as possible. For example, you can create a separate record of the transaction on a spreadsheet and then show them explicitly how their share of the interest from the account is being added to their savings. Deferred gratification now takes tangible, and memorable, form.

As essential as working and playing well with others, knowing how to handle money appropriately is exceedingly important for a child's future happiness.

Full Circle

In many ways, we have come full circle in this book. We began by discussing some psychological predispositions of babies and have ended with the education of children. What have we learned?

The savings problem we are experiencing in the United States is caused partly by psychology that is common to human beings—difficulty deferring gratification, causation-seeking minds, and imperfect memories. The psychology of being an American is also involved; our optimism is rampant. Also contributing are the global economic conditions that have essentially allowed Americans to continue to borrow and that have offered them very low returns on their own savings. These root causes of the savings problem are exacerbated by a culture where wide disparities in wealth and consumption exist. The media are also to blame by constantly providing us with images and stories of others' consumption patterns, be they real or idealized. Furthermore, our market for financial products and services is unclear to many Americans. What can we do about this?

We are not going to change America's basic cultural values. And many of these values have positive consequences as well as negative ones. We must concentrate our efforts where they are likely to yield the highest payoff. With little effort, laws governing disclosure requirements of financial services, particularly those of mutual funds, could change in ways that would have substantial benefits to many Americans who rely on these products for their retirement savings. This is the true low-hanging fruit. In the same vein, business executives could restructure their pension plans to align with the psychological phenomena we have explored here and make savings choices easier for their employees. They could scrutinize their current financial education efforts and take advantage of new changes in federal law. Again, this is not rocket science, nor is it very costly or politically divisive, but it will help.

In the longer term, movements toward taxation that is more consumption-based will alter incentives in ways that favor savings relative to the current system. Allowing poorer Americans access to equity markets via their Social Security contributions is vital for breaking down the financial barriers between the haves and the have-nots.

All of these potential solutions are important. No single one will solve the problem. But we had better get started because while we cannot be sure *when* the consequences of a lack of savings will visit us, we can be sure that they will.

NOTES

Chapter 1: Do Americans Save Too Little?

1. U.S. Department of Commerce, Bureau of Economic Analysis (2006).

2. U.S. Department of the Treasury (1918).

3. Benjamin Disraeli has been credited with offering the opinion that there are three kinds of lies: "lies," "damned lies," and "statistics."

4. See Frank (1999); Twitchell (2002).

5. Research suggests that there is a 15–20% chance that an individual will suffer a work-limiting disability at some point in his or her working life (Chandra and Samwick, 2005).

6. Choi et al. (2004a).

7. See Thaler and Sunstein (2003).

8. Yakoboski (2000).

9. Gale and Sabelhaus (1999).

10. U.S. Department of Commerce, Bureau of Economic Analysis (2006).

11. Harvey (2004).

12. Kahneman and Tversky (1979).

13. Dynan, Skinner, and Zeldes (2004). The results reproduced here are from table 3, page 416, of the referenced article.

14. Friedman (1953).

15. This assumes a 5% draw on your investment income.

16. See Bucks, Kennickell, and Moore (2006) for a detailed analysis of U.S. household ownership of financial assets, including differences among households with various demographic characteristics.

17. Orzechowski and Sepielli (2003).

18. U.S. Department of the Treasury (2006).

19. The enforceability of business contracts and the economic growth it engenders is the subject of numerous articles by the Nobel laureate economist Douglass C. North.

20. Bosworth (2006).

21. This comment is in line with recent trends in hurricane activity.

22. United Technologies is the parent company of Carrier, Pratt & Whitney, Otis Elevator, Sikorsky, Hamilton Sunstrand, and Chubb Fire and Security.

Chapter 2: Why Americans Don't Save Enough

1. Finlay (2005).

2. Ibid.

3. Mann (2005).

4. Ibid.

5. Kamakura, Kossar, and Wedel (2004); Li, Sun, and Wilcox (2005).

6. The quote was taken from the editorial statement of *Marketing Science*, a high-quality academic journal. There are many other journals in marketing that contain articles focusing on the mathematical modeling of consumption choices.

7. Junk e-mail is an entirely different argument. Because there is virtually no cost associated with adding someone to an electronic list, some e-mail that solicits business (particularly for drugs, credit, or sexual aids) can reasonably be described as randomly distributed.

8. Stavins (2000); Aizcorbe, Kennickell, and Moore (2003).

9. See International Labour Organization (2007).

10. Schor (1992), p. 150.

11. Ibid., p. 127.

12. To keep the argument succinct, we have set aside the well-chronicled problems with France's restrictive labor laws.

13. Puri and Robinson (2005) empirically linked optimism about one's economic opportunities with the willingness to work longer hours.

14. It is not possible to find or develop a credible statistic concerning the average number of hours worked by illegal immigrants. Clearly, some of the work goes unreported to the federal government.

15. See Merton and Rossi (1949); Bearden and Etzel (1982); Childers and Rao (1992).

16. Gilovich (1991).

17. DePaulo et al. (1996) examine the frequency of lying in social settings, and Argo, White, and Dahl (2006) study deception in the social exchange of consumption information.

18. The classic book on this topic is Galbraith (1958). More recent examples of authors who have argued that marketing and advertising have contributed to overconsumption are Schor (1998); Frank (1999); Goldman and Papson (2000); and Schwartz (2004).

19. See "Advertising Forecasts" (2006).

20. Veblen (1899).

21. Schor (1998, p. 77) presents evidence from an estimated regression model that those who watch more television save less money. This is used as evidence for the

argument that viewing advertising messages spurs additional consumption. However, it is easy to construct a number of cogent explanations for this that have nothing to do with the impact of advertising.

22. The following analysis relies on the work of Thomas Piketty and Emmanuel Saez.

23. These statistics, as well as figures 2.3 and 2.4, were generated from a publicly available data set provided by Piketty and Saez. The data set is available at http://elsa .berkeley.edu/~saez/TabFig2004prel.xls. For a detailed examination of the methodology used to construct this data set, see Piketty and Saez (2003).

24. Greenspan (2005).

25. See Henslin (1967); Langer and Roth (1975).

26. Langer and Roth (1975).

27. Taylor and Brown (1988); Dobson and Franche (1989).

28. A good reference for the many studies that have been conducted on American optimism can be found in Heine and Lehman (1995).

29. Helprin (1998).

30. Puri and Robinson (2005).

31. Allan Meltzer is the Allan H. Meltzer University Professor of Political Economy at the Tepper School of Business, Carnegie Mellon University. When I asked him about this quote, which I had heard him say many times, he told me that he was probably not the first one to say it, but that he did not remember who was. He is the first person I ever heard say it, and so he is credited.

32. This line of thinking discussed in this section was originally suggested to me by Richard Green, current president of the American Financial Association.

33. See, for example, Bernanke (2005).

34. The mechanism for this transfer of assets is for the government to issue bonds in the local currency, encourage citizens to purchase them, and then use the proceeds of sale to purchase U.S. Treasuries on the open market.

35. The price of a bond and the interest rate offered by a bond are inversely related. For example, if current interest rates were very high, you would be willing to pay less for a bond that matures in several years with a set dollar amount redemption value relative to a situation in which prevailing interest rates were very low. The widespread view among economists as to why governments engage in this behavior is to protect themselves against the kind of currency crises we witnessed in several developing nations in the 1990s. If such a currency crisis did occur, the government could buy their own currency on the open market using their stores of dollar-denominated assets and therefore stem a sudden fall in the value of their home currency.

36. The "real" interest rate is simply the interest rate after subtracting inflation. It is a measure of how the purchasing power of invested money grows.

37. The nominal interest rate was set equal to the yield on a one-year U.S. Treasury bill. We used the Consumer Price Index (CPI) as the measure of inflation. This data is publicly available from the U.S. Federal Reserve Board at http://woodrow.mpls.frb .fed.us/research/data/us/calc/hist1913.cfm.

38. For expository purposes, this analysis ignores any discussion of inflation.

39. And, in fact, some of the dollar figures are ludicrous. Many online calculators are very simplistic in their treatment of your current savings and spending decisions. For example, most calculators consider money you spend on housing, which certainly has investment value, to be the same as money spent on vacations. For that reason, and others, the dollar figures that emerge from these calculators often lack credibility.

40. A good reference for the operational details of mutual funds is Pozen (1998).

41. The history of mutual funds is older than this, see Wilcox (2003), but the widespread adoption of mutual funds is a comparatively recent phenomenon.

42. *2005 Investment Company Fact Book* (2005).

Chapter 3: The Psychology of Money

1. Lusardi and Mitchell (2006). The questions were part of the broader Health Retirement Study, a biannual tracking study conducted by researchers at the University of Michigan. A good overview of the literature on financial literacy can be found in Venti (2005).

2. John Hancock Financial Services (2002).

3. Gustman and Steinmeier (2004).

4. The term "emotional intelligence" was first introduced by Salovey and Mayer (1990) and popularized by Daniel Goleman (1995).

5. Goleman (1995).

6. Gul and Pesendorfer (2001).

7. Bernheim, Skinner, and Weinberg (2001).

8. Ameriks, Caplin, and Leahy (2003).

9. The questions were answered on a scale of 1 to 6, where 1 indicates that the respondent strongly disagrees with the statement and 6 indicates strong agreement.

10. Part of the reason academics engage in this type of research is that there are many examples where the obvious or "commonsense" answer is shown to be completely wrong. This is not one of those cases.

11. Thaler (1986, 1999).

12. Prelec and Lowenstein (1998).

13. Heath, Chatterjee, and France (1995).

14. Thaler (1986).

15. Fischhoff, Slovic, and Lichtenstein (1977).

16. Wright (2000).

17. Shefrin (2000).

18. The "bid" is the price at which an individual can sell a stock, while the "ask" is the price at which he or she can purchase a stock. At any given moment in time, the "ask" for a stock is higher than the "bid," and this spread represents another important trading cost.

19. Odean and Barber (2000); Barber and Odean (2001).

20. Sagan (1996), p. 45. Imitation is the sincerest form of flattery. The title of this section is taken from Nassim Taleb's (2001) book by the same name.

21. This really is the result of flipping a quarter 20 times and writing down the results. This example was suggested to me by a similar one presented in Gilovich (1991).

22. Gilovich, Vallone, and Tversky (1985).

23. J. J. Redick was a celebrated player on the much-loved and much-hated Duke University men's basketball team from 2002–2003 to 2005–2006.

24. For an overview of the literature on persistence in mutual fund performance as well as an analysis of how individual investors consider past performance, see Wilcox (2003).

25. Employee Benefit Research Institute (2006).

26. Gustman and Steinmeier (2004).

27. Hurd and McGarry (1995) found evidence that individuals are able to make reasonable judgments about their likely mortality.

28. For an empirical analysis of the predictions of life-cycle models, see Bernheim, Skinner, and Weinberg (2001). For implications of "exotic preferences" in these models, see Backus, Routledge, and Zin (2004).

29. Although the common preference structure of economic models is "more choice is preferred to less," Gul and Pesendorfer (2001) developed a model in which "temptation," the presence of too many choices, can detract from overall utility.

30. Wright (1975); Hauser and Wernerfelt (1990).

31. Iyengar and Lepper (2000).

32. Iyengar and Jiang (2005).

33. Bernartzi and Thaler (2001).

34. Tversky and Kahneman (1974). At the time of this study, the correct answer to this question was 35%.

35. This story was related to me by Michael Schill, associate professor of business administration at the Darden School.

36. Hastie and Dawes (2001).

37. For an analysis and discussion of why markets can generate very efficient, rational-looking prices, even in the face of considerable irrationality on the part of individual investors, see Gode and Sunder (1993).

38. This is commonly referred to as the "Allais paradox." A good discussion of this paradox can be found in Hastie and Dawes (2001).

39. Savage (1954).

40. The presented example is a somewhat simplified version of the Ellsberg paradox. See Ellsberg (1961).

41. This was calculated from data available at http://www.yahoo.com (Yahoo! Finance). I used monthly data between July 1956 and July 2006, assuming an investment in the Standard & Poor's 500 Index (S&P 500). The data includes both capital appreciation and dividends.

42. Campbell (2006) finds that you are about 30% more likely to hold some equity if you have a college degree.

Chapter 4: Public Policies That Will Increase Savings

1. Widely syndicated talk show host Neil Boortz, a self-described Libertarian, is probably the most widely known advocate of this tax structure.

2. See Chamley (1986); Auerbach and Kotlikoff (1987); Judd (1997); and Atlig et al. (2001).

3. Akst (2006).

4. The USA Tax was an income tax structure that would have exempted all personal savings from federal tax.

5. The Schaefer-Tauzin National Retail Sales Act of 1996 (HR 3039, 104th Congress) proposed replacing the current income tax system with a 15% flat tax on retail sales of goods and services. The Fair Tax Act of 2004 (HR 25, 108th Congress) proposed repealing both income and payroll taxes and substituting a national sales tax of 23%. The Individual Tax Freedom Act of 2004 (HR 4168, 108th Congress) proposed a law similar to the Schaefer-Tauzin act, but included provisions for rebating money to families below specified poverty thresholds.

6. Dynan, Skinner, and Zeldes (2004).

7. The academic literature on the savings effect of shifting to broad-based consumption taxes provides varying estimates of how much savings would increase. For example, Auerbach and Kotlikoff (1987) predict savings increases around 25%, while Engen and Gale (1987) argue that the effect is likely to be much smaller. The critical difference in the predictions between these and similar models is how one expects savings to react to the changes in interest rates that would be generated by such a tax shift. In general, all of these models predict increases in returns to capital and hence an increase in interest rates. If household savings are believed to be relatively sensitive to interest rates, then the savings effect is likely to be large; if they are believed to be relatively insensitive to interest rates, the savings effect, while positive, is likely to be more modest.

8. Lack of data regarding actual behavior under a given proposed policy is a common problem in economic policy analysis. Economic analysis that ignores this potential change in behavior is generally referred to as suffering from the Lucas Critique, named after the economist Robert Lucas. Structural economic modeling attempts to ameliorate the Lucas Critique by exploring individuals' most basic preferences in a way that allows economic prediction even when no behavioral data is present.

9. For a comprehensive examination of the transition issues involved in moving from income to consumption taxes, see Bradford (1996).

10. Copeland (2005).

11. John and Iwry (2006).

12. The fee information in their Blue Chip Value Fund references an agreement that includes the Blue Chip Growth Fund, also managed by Fidelity.

13. Wilcox (2003); Barber, Odean, and Zheng (2005).

14. The expense ratio of a fund is an annualized fee that is expressed as a percent of assets under management.

15. Mahoney (2004) estimates that investors paid about $66 billion in mutual fund fees in 2003.

16. "Mutual Fund Fees" (2000).

17. Letter from Paul Roye, director of the Investment Management Division of the U.S. Securities and Exchange Commission, to Richard Hillman, director of Financial Markets and Community Investment of the U.S. General Accounting Office, April 27, 2001 (http://www.gao.gov/new.items/d01655r.pdf).

18. Wilcox (2001, 2003).

19. An overview of the literature on the persistence of mutual fund performance can be found in Berk and Green (2004).

20. Bogle (1999); Larimore et al. (2006).

21. See Tufano and Sirri (1998) for a discussion of the relationship between past performance, advertising, and mutual fund flows.

22. The rapid flow of monies into a mutual fund after a period of superior performance has been used to explain why fund managers have such difficulty replicating superior performance. The fund manager, upon receipt of the sudden influx of capital, has trouble investing it with the same efficacy as previously held money. See Berk and Green (2004).

23. The 80/20 rule states that 80% of a firm's profits generally come from 20% of its customers.

24. Tufano and Schneider (2005) educated me about the history of U.S. savings bonds. The idea of using savings bonds to help the poor gain better access to capital markets and some of the specifics on how to accomplish this are their ideas as well.

25. This would be a relatively high—though certainly not unheard of—annual management fee for a mutual fund, but a relatively low interest-rate spread for a bank.

26. Li, Sun, and Wilcox (2005) show that a checking account is by far the most frequently purchased service for a new banking customer.

27. Tufano and Schneider (2005).

28. U.S. Department of the Treasury (1918).

29. Gale, Iwry, and Orszag (2005).

30. Duflo et al. (2006).

31. The adjusted gross income of the control group was $43,000, which is similar to the national average.

32. The bulk of this survey was completed in 1995. The authors do address a number of weaknesses with the survey data; most prominent of these is that the survey requires individuals to recollect classroom experiences that occurred many years ago.

33. Someone who does not understand compounding might initially guess 10 years. The answer is about 7.25 years.

Chapter 5: A CEO's Guide to Increasing Employee Savings

1. This is Thaler and Sunstein's (2003) concept of "Libertarian Paternalism."

2. Garman et al. (1999); Burham (2003).

3. This result was derived from a sample of private-sector firms and is the central finding in the doctoral dissertation of Burham (2003).

4. U.S. Department of Labor (http://www.dol.gov).

5. Berk and Green (2004).

6. 12(b)-1 fees are assessed to investors as a way for the fund to recover some of the costs associated with marketing the fund. A good description and examples of the many types of fees that can be leveled by mutual funds can be found in Mahoney (2004).

7. A PDF file of the Uniform Fee Disclosure can be found on the Web site of the U.S. Department of Labor (http://www.dol.gov/ebsa/pdf/401kfefm.pdf).

8. Iyengar and Jiang (2005).

9. Madrian and Shea (2001).

10. Madrian and Shea (2001); Choi et al. (2004b).

11. The Pension Protection Act of 2006.

12. Bernheim and Garrett (2003).

13. Duflo and Saez (2004) found evidence for this positive network effect of financial information, specifically regarding the propensity to enroll in an employer's 401(k) plan.

14. Barber and Odean (2001).

15. Clark et al. (2004).

16. Poterba (2001).

17. Ibid.

18. Very similar to a 401(k) plan, 403(b) is the IRS designation for a tax-deferred savings plan for nonprofit enterprises.

19. Bernartzi and Thaler (2001).

20. In research on a related idea, Ashraf, Karlan, and Yin (2005) present the results of a set of experiments in which individuals could voluntarily instruct a bank not to allow them access to their savings—even if they asked for it. Engaging in this novel type of contracting as a form of self-restraint were people who appeared more likely to exhibit what economists call "time inconsistent preferences," that is, those who have trouble avoiding the temptation of spending money even when they believe that they should not.

21. There is some evidence that similarity in biographical history affects superiors' evaluation of subordinates. Bosses rate employees with similar biographical backgrounds more favorably (Rand and Wexley, 1975). Subordinates who have similar demographic characteristics to their superiors also tend to be rated as more effective employees relative to their counterparts with dissimilar traits (Tsui and O'Reilly, 1989).

22. Bikhchandani, Herschleifer, and Welch (1992). An information cascade forms when people begin to ignore their own preferences and simply follow the behavior of others who have already made such a decision.

Chapter 6: A Household Guide to Saving

1. The term "arbitrage" refers to a financial situation in which an individual can immediately profit at no risk. In general, it is believed that arbitrage opportunities are rare occurrences in modern financial markets.

2. See Damon, Spatt, and Zhang (2004) for an analysis of the amount of money people can and do lose by making this asset-allocation decision incorrectly.

3. Odean and Barber (2000).

4. This psychological tendency not to sell assets that have lost value is called the "disposition effect" in academic literature.

5. For a more detailed explanation, see Wilcox (2001).

6. Bernheim, Garrett, and Maki (1997) found that individuals whose parents were frugal were much more likely themselves to have an above-average propensity to save. This study controlled for other factors that affect savings, such as income and education level.

7. Salovey and Mayer (1990); Goleman (1995).

BIBLIOGRAPHY

"Advertising Forecasts: U.S. Market Trends and Data for All Major Media." (2006). *Kagan Research*, August 17.

Aizcorbe, Ana, Arthur B. Kennickell, and Kevin B. Moore. (2003). "Recent Changes in U.S. Family Finances: Evidence from the 1998 and 2001 Survey of Consumer Finances." *Federal Reserve Bulletin* (January).

Akst, Daniel. (2006). "Long Live the Nanny State." *New York Times*, July 23, sect. 3, p. 3.

Ameriks, John, Andrew Caplin, and John Leahy. (2003). "Wealth Accumulation and the Propensity to Plan." *Quarterly Journal of Economics* (August): 1007–1047.

Argo, Jennifer J., Katherine White, and Darren W. Dahl. (2006). "Social Comparison Theory and Deception in the Interpersonal Exchange of Consumption Information." *Journal of Consumer Research* 33(1): 99–109.

Ashraf, Nava, Dean S. Karlan, and Wesley Yin. (2005). "Tying Odysseus to the Mast: Evidence from a Commitment Savings Product in the Philippines." Working paper, Yale University.

Atlig, David, Alan J. Auerbach, Laurence J. Kotlikoff, Kent A. Smetters, and Jan Walliser. (2001). "Simulating Fundamental Tax Reform in the United States." *American Economic Review* 91(3): 574–595.

Auerbach, Alan J., and Laurence J. Kotlikoff. (1987). *Dynamic Fiscal Policy*. Cambridge: Cambridge University Press.

Backus, David, Bryan Routledge, and Stanley Zin. (2004). "Exotic Preferences for Macroeconomists." National Bureau of Economic Research working paper.

Barber, Brad M., and Terrance Odean. (2001). "Boys Will Be Boys: Gender, Overconfidence, and Common Stock Investment." *Quarterly Journal of Economics* (February): 261–292.

Barber, Brad M., Terrance Odean, and Lu Zheng. (2005). "Out of Sight, Out of Mind: The Effect of Expenses on Mutual Fund Flows." *Journal of Business* 78(6): 2095–2119.

Bearden, William O., and Michael J. Etzel. (1982). "Reference Group Influence on Product and Brand Purchase Decisions." *Journal of Consumer Research* 9(4): 183–194.

Berk, Jonathan B., and Richard C. Green. (2004). "Mutual Fund Flows and Performance in Rational Markets." *Journal of Political Economy* 112(6): 1269–1295.

Bernanke, Ben S. (2005). "The Global Saving Glut and the U.S. Current Account Deficit." Remarks before the Virginia Association of Economics, Richmond, March 10.

Bernartzi, Shlomo, and Richard H. Thaler. (2001). "Naïve Diversification Strategies in Defined Contribution Savings Plans." *American Economic Review* 91(1): 79–98.

Bernheim, Douglas, and Daniel Garrett. (2003). "The Effects of Financial Education in the Workplace: Evidence from a Survey of Households." *Journal of Public Economics* 87: 1487–1519.

Bernheim, Douglas, Jonathan Skinner, and Steven Weinberg. (2001). "What Accounts for the Variation in Retirement Wealth among U.S. Households?" *American Economic Review* 91: 832–857.

Bernheim, Douglas B., Daniel M. Garrett, and Dean M. Maki. (1997). "Education and Saving: The Long-Term Effects of High School Financial Curriculum Mandates." National Bureau of Economic Research working paper no. 6085, July.

Bikhchandani, Sushil, David Herschleifer, and Ivo Welch. (1992). "A Theory of Fads, Fashion, Custom and Cultural Change as Information Cascades." *Journal of Political Economy* 100: 992–1026.

Bogle, John C. (1994). *Bogle on Mutual Funds: New Perspectives for the Intelligent Investor*. New York: Dell.

———. (1999). *Common Sense on Mutual Funds*. New York: John Wiley & Sons.

Bosworth, Barry P. (2006). "United States Savings in a Global Context." Remarks before the United States Senate Committee on Finance, April 6.

Bradford, David F. (1996). "Consumption Taxes: Some Fundamental Transition Issues." National Bureau of Economic Research working paper no. 5290.

Bucks, Brian K., Arthur B. Kennickell, and Kevin B. Moore. (2006). "Recent Changes in U.S. Family Finances: Evidence from the 2001 and 2004 Survey of Consumer Finances." *Federal Reserve Bulletin* 92: A1–A38.

Burham, Kim. (2003). "401(k)s as a Strategic Compensation: Align Pay with Productivity and Enable Optimal Separation." Ph.D. dissertation, University of Notre Dame, June.

Campbell, John Y. (2006). "Household Finance." Presidential Address to the American Finance Association, January 7.

Chamley, Christophe. (1986). "Optimal Taxation of Capital Income in General Equilibrium with Infinite Lives." *Econometrica* 54(3): 607–622.

Chandra, Amitabh, and Andrew A. Samwick. (2005). "Disability Risk and the Value of Disability Insurance." National Bureau of Economic Research working paper no. 11605.

Childers, Terry L., and Akshay R. Rao. (1992). "The Influence of Familial and Peer-Based Reference Groups on Consumer Decisions." *Journal of Consumer Research* 19(2): 198–211.

Choi, James, Brigitte Madrian, Andrew Metrick, and David Laibson. (2004a). "For Better or for Worse: Default Effects and 401(k) Savings Behavior." In David Wise (ed.), *Perspectives in the Economics of Aging*. Chicago: University of Chicago Press, pp. 81–121.

Choi, James J., David Laibson, Brigitte Madrian, and Andrew Metrick. (2004b). "Optimal Defaults and Active Decisions: Theory and Evidence from 401(k) Saving." Working paper, Harvard University.

Clark, Robert, Madeleine D'Ambrosio, Ann McDermed, and Kshama Sawant. (2004). "Sex Differences, Financial Education, and Retirement Goals." In Olivia Mitchell and Stephen Utkus (eds.), *Pension Design and Structure: New Lessons from Behavioral Finance*. Oxford: Oxford University Press, pp. 185–206.

Copeland, Craig. (2005). "Employer-Based Retirement Plan Participation: Geographic Differences and Trends." Employee Benefit Research Institute, Issue Brief no. 286.

Damon, Robert M., Chester S. Spatt, and Harold H. Zhang. (2004). "Optimal Asset Location and Allocation with Taxable and Tax-Deferred Investing." *Journal of Finance* 59(3): 999–1038.

DePaulo, Bella M., Deborah A. Kashy, Susan E. Kirkendol, Melissa M. Wyer, and Jennifer A. Epstein. (1996). "Lying in Everyday Life." *Journal of Personality and Social Psychology* 70 (May): 970–995.

Dobson, K., and R. L. Franche. (1989). "A Conceptual and Empirical Review of the Depressive Realism Hypothesis." *Canadian Journal of Behavioral Science* 21: 419–433.

Duflo, Esther, William Gale, Jeffrey Lieberman, Peter Orzag, and Emmanuel Saez. (2006). "Saving Incentives for Low- and Middle-Income Families: Evidence from a Field Experiment with H&R Block." *Quarterly Journal of Economics* 121(4): 1311–1346. (See also National Bureau of Economic Research working paper no. 11680, 2005.)

Duflo, Esther, and Emmanuel Saez. (2004). "Implications of Pension Plan Features, Information, and Social Interactions for Retirement Saving Decisions." In Olivia Mitchell and Stephen Utkus (eds.), *Pension Design and Structure: New Lessons from Behavioral Finance*. Oxford: Oxford University Press, pp. 137–155.

Dynan, Karen E., Jonathan Skinner, and Stephen P. Zeldes. (2004). "Do the Rich Save More?" *Journal of Political Economy* 112(21): 397–444.

Ellsberg, D. (1961). "Risk, Ambiguity, and the Savage Axioms." *Quarterly Journal of Economics* 75: 643–669.

Employee Benefit Research Institute. (2006). "Retirement Plans and Retirement Confidence in Higher Education." *Notes* 27(3): 2–5.

Engen, Eric M., and William G. Gale. (1987). "Consumption Taxes and Savings: The Role of Uncertainty in Tax Reform." *American Economic Review* 87(2): 114–119.

Fair Tax Act of 2003. (2003). HR 25, 108th Congress. GovTrack.us (database of federal legislation). http://www.govtrack.us/congress/bill.xpd?bill=h108-25 (accessed November 19, 2007).

Fenton-O'Creevy, M., N. Nicholson, E. Soane, and P. Willman. (2003). "Trading on Illusions: Unrealistic Perceptions of Control and Trading Performance." *Journal of Occupational and Organizational Psychology* 76: 53–68.

Finlay, Steven. (2005). *Consumer Credit Fundamentals*. London: Palgrave Macmillan.

Fischhoff, B., P. Slovic, and S. Lichtenstein. (1977). "Knowing with Certainty: The Appropriateness of Extreme Confidence." *Journal of Experimental Psychology: Human Perception and Performance* 3: 552–564.

Frank, Robert H. (1999). *Luxury Fever*. New York: Free Press.

Friedman, Milton. (1953). "Choice, Chance, and the Personal Distribution of Income." *Journal of Political Economy* 61 (August): 277–290.

———. (1962). *Capitalism and Freedom*. Chicago: University of Chicago Press.

———. (1980). *Free to Choose*. New York: Harcourt Brace Jovanovich.

Galbraith, John Kenneth. (1958). *The Affluent Society*. Boston: Houghton Mifflin.

Gale, William G., J. Mark Iwry, and Peter R. Orszag. (2005). "The Saver's Credit: Expanding Retirement Savings for Middle- and Lower-Income Americans." Retirement Security Project Brief no. 2005-2. Washington, DC: The Retirement Security Project.

Gale, William G., and John Sabelhaus. (1999). "Perspectives on the Household Savings Rate." *Brookings Papers on Economic Activity* 1: 181–224.

Garman, E. Thomas, Jinhee Kim, Constance Y. Kratzer, Bruce H. Brunson, and So-Hyun Joo. (1999). "Workplace Financial Education Improves Personal Financial Wellness." *Association for Financial Counseling and Planning Education* 10(1): 79–88.

Gilovich, Thomas. (1991). *How We Know What Isn't So*. New York: Free Press.

Gilovich, Thomas, Robert Vallone, and Amos Tversky. (1985). "The Hot Hand in Basketball: On the Misperceptions of Random Sequences." *Cognitive Psychology* 17: 295–314.

Gode, Dhananjay K., and Shyam Sunder. (1993). "Allocative Efficiency of Markets with Zero Intelligence Traders: Market as a Partial Substitute for Individual Rationality." *Journal of Political Economy* 101(1): 119–137.

Goldman, Robert, and Stephen Papson. (2000). "Advertising in the Age of Accelerated Meaning." In Juliet Schor and Douglas B. Holt (eds.), *The Consumer Society Reader*. New York: New Press, pp. 1–98.

Goleman, Daniel. (1995). *Emotional Intelligence: Why It Can Matter More Than IQ*. New York: Bantam Books.

Greenspan, Alan. (2005). Testimony before the U.S. House of Representatives Committee on Financial Services, July 30.

Gul, Faruk, and Wolfgang Pesendorfer. (2001). "Temptation and Self-Control." *Econometrica* 69: 1403–1449.

Gustman, Alan, and Thomas Steinmeier. (2004). "What People Don't Know about Their Pensions and Social Security." In W. Gale and J. Shoven (eds.), *Public Policies and Private Pensions*. Washington, DC: Brookings Institution, pp. 57–119.

Harvey, Ross. (2004). "Comparison of Household Saving Ratios: Euro Area/United States/Japan." OECD Statistics Brief no. 8. Paris: Organisation for Economic Co-operation and Development. http://www.oecd.org/dataoecd/53/48/32023442.pdf (accessed November 19, 2007).

Hastie, Reid, and Robyn M. Dawes. (2001). *Rational Choice in an Uncertain World*. Thousand Oaks, CA: Sage Publications.

Hauser, John R., and Berger Wernerfelt. (1990). "An Evaluation Cost Model of Consideration Sets." *Journal of Consumer Research* 16: 393–408.

Heath, T. B., S. Chatterjee, and K. R. France. (1995). "Mental Accounting and Changes in Price: The Frame Dependence of Reference Dependence." *Journal of Consumer Research* 22 (June): 90–97.

Heine, S. J., and D. R. Lehman. (1995). "Cultural Variation in Unrealistic Optimism: Does the West Feel More Invulnerable than the East?" *Journal of Personality and Social Psychology* 68: 595–607.

Helprin, Mark. (1998). "Statesmanship and Its Betrayal." *Wall Street Journal*, July 2, p. A22.

Henslin, J. M. (1967). "Craps and Magic." *American Journal of Sociology* 73: 316–330.

Hurd, Michael, and Kathleen McGarry. (1995). "Evaluation of Subjective Probabilities of Survival in the Health and Retirement Study." *Journal of Human Resources* 30: S268–S292.

Individual Tax Freedom Act of 2004. (2004). HR 4168, 108th Congress. GovTrack.us (database of federal legislation). http://www.govtrack.us/congress/bill.xpd?bill=h108-4168 (accessed November 19, 2007).

International Labour Organization. (2007). "Key Indicators of the Labour Market." http://www.ilo.org/public/english/employment/strat/kilm/kilm06.htm.

Iyengar, Sheena S., and Wei Jiang. (2005). "The Psychological Cost of Ever Increasing Choice: A Fallback to the Sure Bet." Working paper, Columbia University.

Iyengar, Sheena S., and Mark R. Lepper. (2000). "When Choice Is Demotivating: Can One Desire Too Much of a Good Thing?" *Journal of Personality and Social Psychology* 79(6): 995–1006.

John, David C., and J. Mark Iwry. (2006). "Increasing Retirement Security through Automatic IRAs." Testimony before the Subcommittee on Long-Term Growth and the Debt Reduction Committee on Finance, United States Senate, June 29.

John Hancock Financial Services. (2002). *Eighth Annual Defined Contribution Survey*. Boston: John Hancock Financial Services.

Judd, Kenneth L. (1997). "The Optimal Tax Rate for Capital Income Is Negative." National Bureau of Economic Research working paper no. 6004, April.

Kahneman, Daniel, and Amos Tversky. (1979). "Prospect Theory: An Analysis of Decision under Risk." *Econometrica* 47 (March): 263–291.

Kamakura, Wagner, Bruce Kossar, and Michael Wedel. (2004). "Identifying Innovators for the Cross-Selling of New Products." *Management Science* 50(8): 1120–1133.

Langer, E. J., and J. Roth. (1975). "Heads I Win, Tails It's Chance: The Illusion of Control as a Function of the Sequence of Outcomes in a Purely Chance Task." *Journal of Personality and Social Psychology* 34: 191–198.

Larimore, Taylor, Mel Lindauer, Michael LeBoeuf, and John C. Bogle. (2006). *The Boglehead's Guide to Investing*. Hoboken, NJ: John Wiley & Sons.

Li, Shibo, Baohong Sun, and Ronald T. Wilcox. (2005). "Cross-Selling Naturally Ordered Services: An Application to Consumer Banking Services." *Journal of Marketing Research* 42 (May): 233–239.

Lusardi, Annamaria, and Olivia S. Mitchell. (2006). "Financial Literacy and Planning: Implications for Retirement Well-Being." Michigan Retirement Research Center working paper no. 2005-108.

Madrian, Brigitte, and Dennis Shea. (2001). "The Power of Suggestion: Inertia in 401(k) Participation and Savings Behavior." *Quarterly Journal of Economics* 116(4): 1149–1187.

Mahoney, Paul G. (2004). "Manager-Investor Conflicts in Mutual Funds." *Journal of Economic Perspectives* 18(2): 161–182.

Mann, Ronald J. (2005). "Global Credit Card Use and Debt: Policy Issues and Regulatory Responses." University of Texas Law and Economics Research Paper no. 49.

Mencken, H. L. (1917). "The Divine Afflatus." *New York Evening Mail*, November 16.

Merton, Robert K., and Alice Kitti Rossi. (1949). "Contributions to the Theory of Reference Group Behavior." In Robert K. Merton (ed.), *Social Theory and Social Structure*. New York: Free Press, pp. 225–275.

"Mutual Fund Fees: Additional Disclosure Could Encourage Price Competition." (2000). Report to the Chairman, Subcommittee on Finance and Hazardous Materials, and the Ranking Member, Committee on Commerce, House of Representatives, June. GAO/GGD-00-126. http://www.gao.gov/archive/2000/gg00126.pdf (accessed November 19, 2007).

National Oceanic and Atmospheric Administration. (2006). "NOAA Predicts Very Active 2006 North Atlantic Hurricane Season." May 22. http://www.publicaffairs.noaa.gov/releases2006/may06/noaa06-056.html (accessed November 19, 2007).

National Retail Sales Tax Act of 1996. (1996). HR 3039, 104th Congress. GovTrack.us (database of federal legislation). http://www.govtrack.us/congress/bill.xpd?bill=h104-3039 (accessed November 19, 2007).

Odean, Terrance, and Brad M. Barber. (2000). "Trading Is Hazardous to Your Wealth: The Common Stock Investment Performance of Individual Investors." *Journal of Finance* 55(2): 773–806.

Orzechowski, Shawna, and Peter Sepielli. (2003). "Net Worth and Asset Ownership of Households: 1998 and 2000." *U.S. Census Bureau Current Population Reports* (May): 70–88.

Pension Protection Act of 2006. (2006). HR 4, 109th Congress. GovTrack.us (database of federal legislation). http://www.govtrack.us/congress/bill.xpd?bill=h109-4 (accessed November 19, 2007).

Piketty, Thomas, and Emmanuel Saez. (2003). "Income Inequality in the United States: 1913–1998." *Quarterly Journal of Economics* 118(1): 1–39.

Poterba, James. (2001). "A Brief History of Annuity Markets." In Jeffrey Brown, Olivia S. Mitchell, and James Poterba (eds.), *The Role of Annuity Markets in Enhancing Retirement*. Cambridge, MA: MIT Press, pp. 23–56.

Pozen, Robert C. (1998). *The Mutual Fund Business*. Cambridge, MA: MIT Press.

Prelec, D., and George Lowenstein. (1998). "The Red and the Black: Mental Accounting of Savings and Debt." *Marketing Science* 17: 4–28.

Puri, Manju, and David Robinson. (2005). "Optimism and Economic Choice." National Bureau of Economic Research working paper no. 11361.

Rand, Thomas M., and Kenneth N. Wexley. (1975). "Demonstration of the Effect, 'Similar to Me,' in Simulated Employee Interviews." *Psychological Reports* 36(2): 535–544.

Sagan, Carl. (1996). *The Demon-Haunted World*. New York: Random House.

Salovey, P., and J. D. Mayer. (1990). "Emotional Intelligence." *Imagination, Cognition, and Personality* 9: 185–211.

Savage, Leonard J. (1954). *The Foundations of Statistics*. New York: John Wiley.

Schor, Juliet. (1992). *The Overworked American: The Unexpected Decline of Leisure*. New York: Basic Books.

———. (1998). *The Overspent American: Why We Want What We Don't Need*. New York: HarperPerennial.

Schwartz, Barry. (2004). *The Paradox of Choice: Why More Is Less*. New York: Basic Books.

Shefrin, Hersch. (2000). *Beyond Greed and Fear: Behavioral Finance and the Psychology of Investing*. Oxford: Oxford University Press.

Stavins, Joanna. (2000). "Credit Card Borrowing, Delinquency, and Personal Bankruptcy." *New England Economic Review* (July/August): 15–30.

Taleb, Nassim Nicholas. (2001). *Fooled by Randomness*. New York: W. W. Norton.

Taylor, S. E., and J. D. Brown. (1988). "Illusion and Well-Being—A Social Psychological Perspective on Mental Health." *Psychological Bulletin* 103(2): 193–210.

Thaler, Richard. (1986). "Mental Accounting and Consumer Choice." *Marketing Science* 4(3): 199–214.

———. (1999). "Mental Accounting Matters." *Journal of Behavioral Decision Making* 12(3): 183–206

Thaler, Richard H., and Cass R. Sunstein. (2003). "Libertarian Paternalism." *The American Economic Review* 93(2): 175–179.

Tsui, Anne S., and Charles A. O'Reilly. (1989). "Beyond Simple Demographic Effects: The Importance of Relational Demography in Superior–Subordinate Dyads." *Academy of Management Journal* 32(2): 402–423.

Tufano, Peter, and Daniel Schneider. (2005). "Reinventing Savings Bonds." Working paper, Harvard Business School.

Tufano, Peter, and Erik Sirri. (1998). "Costly Search and Mutual Fund Flows." *Journal of Finance* 53: 1589–1622.

Tversky, Amos, and Daniel Kahneman. (1974). "Judgements under Uncertainty: Heuristics and Biases." *Science* 185: 1124–1131.

Twitchell, James B. (2002). *America's Love Affair with Luxury*. New York: Simon and Schuster.

2005 Investment Company Fact Book. (2005). Washington, DC: Investment Company Institute.

U.S. Department of Commerce. Bureau of Economic Analysis. (2006). "Table 5.1: Savings and Investment." National Income and Product Accounts. Washington, DC: U.S. Department of Commerce.

U.S. Department of Labor. (2004). "Understanding Retirement Fees and Expenses." Washington, DC: U.S. Department of Labor, May.

U.S. Department of the Treasury. (1918). *To Make Thrift a Happy Habit*. Washington, DC: U.S. Department of the Treasury.

———. (2006). "Major Foreign Holders of U.S. Treasury Securities." Washington, DC: U.S. Department of the Treasury, January.

Veblen, Thorstein. (1899). *The Theory of the Leisure Class: An Economic Study in the Evolution of Institutions*. New York: Macmillan.

Venti, Steven F. (2005). "Choice, Behavior and Retirement Savings." In Gordon Clark, Alicia Munnell, and Michael Orszag (eds.), *Oxford Handbook of Pensions and Retirement Income*. New York: Oxford University Press, pp. 603–617.

Wilcox, Ronald T. (2001). "Advertising Mutual Fund Returns: A Critical Analysis of a U.S. Securities and Exchange Commission Proposal to Change Advertising Law." *Journal of Public Policy & Marketing* 20(1): 133–137.

———. (2003). "Bargain Hunting or Star Gazing: How Investors Choose Mutual Funds." *Journal of Business* 76(4): 645–663.

Wright, P. (1975). "Consumer Choice Strategies: Simplifying vs. Optimizing." *Journal of Marketing Research* 12: 60–67.

Wright, Robert. (1994). *The Moral Animal*. New York: Random House.

———. (2000). *NonZero: The Logic of Human Destiny*. New York: Vintage Books.

Yakoboski, P. (2000). "Retirement Plans, Personal Saving, and Saving Adequacy." Employee Benefit Research Institute Issue Brief no. 219, March.

INDEX

Note: *Italicized* page numbers indicate figures or tables.